Pennsylvania Legal Research

Carolina Academic Press
Legal Research Series

Suzanne E. Rowe, Series Editor
Tenielle Fordyce-Ruff, Associate Series Editor

❧

Arizona, Second Edition—Tamara S. Herrera

Arkansas, Second Edition—Coleen M. Barger, Cheryl L. Reinhart & Cathy L. Underwood

California, Third Edition—Aimee Dudovitz, Hether C. Macfarlane, & Suzanne E. Rowe

Colorado—Robert Michael Linz

Connecticut—Jessica G. Hynes

Federal, Second Edition—Mary Garvey Algero, Spencer L. Simons, Suzanne E. Rowe, Scott Childs & Sarah E. Ricks

Florida, Fourth Edition—Barbara J. Busharis, Jennifer LaVia & Suzanne E. Rowe

Georgia—Nancy P. Johnson, Elizabeth G. Adelman & Nancy J. Adams

Idaho, Second Edition—Tenielle Fordyce-Ruff & Kristina J. Running

Illinois, Second Edition—Mark E. Wojcik

Iowa, Second Edition—John D. Edwards, Karen L. Wallace & Melissa H. Weresh

Kansas—Joseph A. Custer & Christopher L. Steadham

Kentucky, Second Edition—William A. Hilyerd, Kurt X. Metzmeier & David J. Ensign

Louisiana, Second Edition—Mary Garvey Algero

Massachusetts, Second Edition—E. Joan Blum & Shaun B. Spencer

Michigan, Third Edition—Pamela Lysaght & Cristina D. Lockwood

Minnesota—Suzanne Thorpe

Mississippi—Kristy L. Gilliland

Missouri, Third Edition—Wanda M. Temm & Julie M. Cheslik

New York, Third Edition—Elizabeth G. Adelman, Theodora Belniak, Courtney L. Selby & Brian Detweiler

North Carolina, Second Edition—Scott Childs & Sara Sampson

North Dakota—Anne Mullins & Tammy Pettinato

Ohio, Second Edition—Sara Sampson, Katherine L. Hall & Carolyn Broering-Jacobs

Oklahoma—Darin K. Fox, Darla W. Jackson & Courtney L. Selby

Oregon, Third Edition Revised Printing—Suzanne E. Rowe

Pennsylvania, Second Edition—Barbara J. Busharis, Catherine M. Dunn, Bonny L. Tavares & Carla P. Wale

Tennessee, Second Edition—Scott Childs, Sibyl Marshall & Carol McCrehan Parker

Texas, Second Edition—Spencer L. Simons

Washington, Second Edition—Julie Heintz-Cho, Tom Cobb & Mary A. Hotchkiss

West Virginia—Hollee Schwartz Temple

Wisconsin—Patricia Cervenka & Leslie Behroozi

Wyoming, Second Edition—Debora A. Person & Tawnya K. Plumb

❧

Pennsylvania Legal Research

Second Edition

Barbara J. Busharis
Catherine M. Dunn
Bonny L. Tavares
Carla P. Wale

Suzanne E. Rowe, Series Editor
Tenielle Fordyce-Ruff, Associate Series Editor

CAROLINA ACADEMIC PRESS
Durham, North Carolina

Library of Congress Cataloging-in-Publication Data

Names: Busharis, Barbara J., 1962- author. | Dunn, Catherine M., author. | Tavares, Bonny L., author. | Wale, Carla P., author.
Title: Pennsylvania legal research / Barbara J. Busharis, Catherine M. Dunn, Bonny L. Tavares, Carla P. Wale.
Description: Second edition. | Durham, North Carolina : Carolina Academic Press, LLC, [2017] | Series: Carolina Academic Press legal research series | Includes bibliographical references and index.
Identifiers: LCCN 2017022436 | ISBN 9781531007522 (alk. paper)
Subjects: LCSH: Legal research--Pennsylvania.
Classification: LCC KFP75 .B87 2017 | DDC 340.072/0748--dc23
LC record available at https://lccn.loc.gov/2017022436

eISBN 978-1-53100-753-9

Carolina Academic Press, LLC
700 Kent Street
Durham, North Carolina 27701
Telephone (919) 489-7486
Fax (919) 493-5668
www.cap-press.com

Printed in the United States of America

Summary of Contents

Contents

List of Tables and Figures

Tables

Figures

Series Note

The Legal Research Series published by Carolina Academic Press includes titles from many states around the country as well as a separate text on federal legal research. The goal of each book is to provide law students, practitioners, paralegals, college students, laypeople, and librarians with the essential elements of legal research in each jurisdiction. Unlike more bibliographic texts, the Legal Research Series books seek to explain concisely both the sources of legal research and the process for conducting legal research effectively.

Preface and Acknowledgments

This is the second edition of a book originally published in 2007. The primary audience for the book is law students who are preparing to practice law in Pennsylvania, but the book is intended to be helpful to anyone who needs a practical introduction to legal research, with a focus on Pennsylvania sources. This wider audience may include students in other disciplines, professionals, and even people representing themselves in Pennsylvania courts. Researchers who have already learned the basics of legal research, but who are not familiar with unique features of Pennsylvania law, will also find this book a handy reference.

Since the first edition was published, electronic legal research has become dominant, and online sources of legal authority and analysis have increased exponentially. Thus, although the organization of this book is similar in many respects to the first edition, the focus has changed from describing print and online alternatives to describing the most efficient research methods for particular types of authority.

The second edition still begins with a general overview of the research process and research methods. Primary sources are covered next. While we debated beginning with secondary sources to emphasize their role as starting points for further research, we decided to use a chapter order that reinforces the priority of finding primary authorities. However, research courses that begin with secondary authorities can easily assign those chapters first. The original chapter on Secondary Sources has been expanded and divided into two chapters, Secondary Sources and Practice Aids. This division allowed us to expand coverage of these sources, and at the same time to reinforce the distinctions between those sources that might be cited as persuasive authority in a memo or brief, and those that are especially useful as springboards for further research. At the end of the book, an Appendix provides practical guidance on incorporating legal citations into documents, and highlights citation issues that frequently arise when citing Pennsylvania sources.

This edition benefitted tremendously from the addition of two co-authors, Catherine Dunn and Carla Wale, whose research and teaching expertise added valuable insights. We are indebted to those who helped develop the first edition, including other authors in the Carolina Academic Press Legal Research Series. We are also heavily indebted to the many students who have given us feedback on the first edition over the years.

Pennsylvania Legal Research

Chapter 1

The Legal Research Process

This book will teach you to be a better researcher of Pennsylvania law. This is true whether you are new to legal research or a seasoned researcher. This book describes the core legal research resources available in Pennsylvania, and it details the research methods available for accessing them efficiently and effectively. It also includes brief explanations of federal research, when appropriate, to introduce additional resources or highlight differences between state and federal law. These differences are minor, however, as the fundamentals of legal research are the same in every American jurisdiction.

I. The Intersection of Legal Research and Legal Analysis

Legal analysis is interwoven throughout the legal research process. Every legal research project begins with an analysis of the relevant issues. This includes questions such as:

- What are the important facts?
- What is the relevant jurisdiction?
- What do you know already about this area of law?
- Which search terms might be helpful?
- What type of authority is most likely to govern the issue?

Practical issues also need to be considered:

- Which type of research method will you try first?
- What are the time limitations for this project?
- How were you asked to present your findings?

This type of preliminary analysis allows you to make informed decisions about the materials you will use and how you plan to use them. As with other types of research in the digital age, it is all too easy to fall victim to information overload when conducting legal research. Taking the time to do a thoughtful initial analysis of these types of threshold questions will help reduce the time you spend spinning your wheels later on in the process.

This preliminary analysis is only the beginning of the intersection of research and analysis in the legal research process. You will use legal analysis throughout the research process as you learn more about your legal issues, adjust your research process accordingly, update your findings, and ultimately decide which legal materials best meet your needs for a given legal research project. This includes reasoning by analogy, which legal argument often requires.

II. Types and Weight of Legal Authority

Your primary goal as a legal researcher is to find all of the binding or controlling authority on your legal issues. Law is unique in that your research must be comprehensive. You must endeavor to find *all* relevant binding authority and reference it, whether or not it supports your position on the legal issue you are researching. If you find binding authority that does not support your position, your role is to analyze it and distinguish it, if at all possible. In fact, the Rules of Professional Conduct in Pennsylvania expressly prohibit a lawyer from failing to disclose adverse legal authority not cited to by opposing counsel. Both the Pennsylvania Rules of Civil Procedure and the Federal Rules of Civil Procedure require that the claims, defenses, and other legal contentions in a court pleading must be warranted by existing law or by a non-frivolous argument for modifying or extending the law.[1]

As a starting point in considering the types and weight of legal authority, note that there are *primary sources* and *secondary sources*, and only primary sources can be binding authority. Primary sources are authorized statements of the law issued by government bodies with lawmaking power, and they include materials such as constitutions, statutes, cases, regulations, administrative decisions, and evidentiary and procedural rules. You will find detailed information about each type of primary source and how to find it in the subsequent chapters in this book.

Secondary sources include everything else. They are writings about the law, rather than the law itself. Secondary sources cover a wide spectrum, from very

---

1. Pennsylvania Rule of Professional Conduct 3.3(a)(2) explains the duty of candor towards the court. The responsibility of an advocate when drafting pleadings is set out in Pennsylvania Rule of Civil Procedure 1023.1(c)(2), which mirrors Federal Rule of Civil Procedure 11(b)(2).

Table 1-1. Examples of Authority in Pennsylvania Research

	Mandatory Authority	Persuasive Authority
Primary Authority	Pennsylvania statutes Pennsylvania Supreme Court decisions	Interpretations of similar Delaware statutes New Jersey Supreme Court decisions
Secondary Authority		Law review articles A practice-oriented treatise focusing on a specific area of Pennsylvania law

sophisticated to very simple, and they aid in understanding the law and locating citations to relevant primary authority.

Only primary sources can be binding authority, but they must be *mandatory authority*, rather than *persuasive authority*, to be binding. A determination as to which legal materials constitute mandatory authority in a given research area is based upon the relationship of lawmaking bodies to each other in a particular jurisdiction, as well as the level of similarity between the legal materials you located and the relevant issues and facts in your research project. Broadly speaking, relevant statutes and regulations in your jurisdiction constitute mandatory authority, and higher courts bind lower courts within that jurisdiction.

Persuasive authority includes primary legal materials from different jurisdictions or lower courts within your jurisdiction, as well as legal materials not produced by a lawmaking body. Even though persuasive authority is non-binding, courts may follow it if it is relevant and well-reasoned. Courts are more likely to rely on persuasive authority if mandatory authority is absent in a given jurisdiction or if it is incomplete, outdated, or in opposition to a notable number of other jurisdictions.

III. The Research Process

A skillful approach to legal research requires following a process or framework designed to ensure efficient and effective research. This structure leads to both binding and persuasive authority on a given legal issue as well as commentary to help analyze it. The exact research process or strategy may differ

Table 1-2. Overview of the Research Process

1. Develop a *research plan* and generate a list of *research terms*.
2. Consult *secondary sources* and practice materials.
3. Determine whether the issue is controlled by a *constitutional provision*, *statute*, or *regulation*. If so, find the controlling provisions and cases that interpret or apply them.
4. Find *cases* on point; determine whether they are binding or persuasive.
5. *Update* all primary authorities to ensure they have not been repealed, reversed, modified, or otherwise changed.

---

from one researcher to another, as well as from one research project to another, but your research results will be more consistent if you use a framework for your research.

A suggested process is described below and outlined in Table 1-2. This basic process can be customized for each research project. If you are unfamiliar with an area of law, you should follow each step of the process in the order indicated. Keep in mind that none of the steps are ever truly "completed" until you reach a point where you are comfortable stopping. A secondary source may provide additional research terms; a judicial opinion may cite to a statute or administrative rule you had not considered; and updating your primary authorities may reveal additional primary authorities not included in your original results. This is all a normal part of the research process.

The first step is developing a research plan and generating a list of research terms. This list of terms will become your launching point, whether you are researching online or using print sources. Try to think of potential synonyms for each of your terms. This is especially important for online research. If you are looking for a law requiring booster seats for children under a certain age, and the law actually refers to "child safety seats," you may not find it right away.

Next, consult one or more secondary sources to provide context for the issue you are researching. Especially when you are researching an unfamiliar area, doing background reading in secondary sources will help you identify how your issue fits into that area in general. This, in turn, lessens the chance that you will frame the issue too narrowly or too broadly. Secondary sources can also help you identify whether there is something unique about that issue in your jurisdiction, and can help you develop or anticipate additional arguments. Finally, secondary sources often lead to citations to primary authority.

The next step, which will be answered in part by your reading in secondary sources, is to determine whether some combination of constitutional provisions, statutes, or regulations will govern the resolution of your issue. If so, find those provisions and analyze their terms. Then, using the tools provided in many statutory research sources, find cases or agency decisions interpreting and applying the provisions. Unless the scope of your research is limited at the outset — for example, when you are asked to find out whether any amendments to a particular statute are pending — your research will require consulting more than one type of primary authority.

Many novice researchers believe they should begin their research with cases rather than statutes and regulations. In actuality, the law made by legislatures (statutes) and administrative agencies (regulations) is much more complete in some areas of the law than the law handed down in judicial decisions. This is partly because certain areas are highly legislated and regulated, such as environmental law, and partly because many disputes never reach the appellate level, and so do not result in a judicial opinion that can be relied upon as binding authority. Statutes and regulations also tend to be organized in a user-friendly way, by topic. In addition, both in print and online, annotated versions of statutes (and, to a lesser extent, administrative codes) will take you directly to other, related primary authorities once you have found a controlling statutory provision.

If there is no controlling constitutional, statutory, or regulatory provision, or if you cannot locate decisions on point by using statutory research materials, the next step will be to use case-finding tools, such as the headnote system, a citator, or full-text searches, to find applicable cases. As you locate cases, you will need to pay close attention to whether they are binding or merely persuasive.

The final step is updating. The word "updating" has both a broad and a narrower connotation in legal research. In the narrow sense, it is used to refer to the process of determining whether a specific primary source has any negative history. This is done using a citator (Shepard's on Lexis Advance and KeyCite on Westlaw).[2] Your research is not complete until you have specifically updated each of the primary authorities on which you rely. Each of the chapters in this book that covers a specific type of source includes information on updating your research.

---

2. *Shepard's Citations* was the earliest and, for a time, the most-used citator in legal research, so practicing attorneys still often refer to all citators as "Shepard's." If you are asked to "Shepardize" a statute but you use Westlaw, simply use KeyCite.

In the broader sense, however, updating means doing thorough enough re-search to ensure that you are basing your analysis on a current and accurate view of the law, not just making sure that a specific source is still "good law." One example of insufficient updating would be updating a specific statutory provision using only legislative materials, such as recent session laws affecting that provision, without also looking to see how the statute has been treated in administrative regulations and judicial opinions. Finding recent legislative modifications to a statute will not tell you whether a portion of that statute has been declared unconstitutional by a state court. The most recent annotated version of the statute may give you that information, or may need further up-dating itself (through looking at very recent court decisions), before you can be comfortable that the statute is still "good law."

Your research is complete when you have looked for each type of primary legal material using a variety of different research methods; you have deter-mined what primary authority is controlling (or, in some situations, that no controlling authorities exist); and you keep coming across the same authorities. Even then, as you begin to write a memo or brief based on your research, the writing process may reveal gaps or additional issues. In that case, you will circle back to an earlier step in the process and continue until the gaps are filled.

IV. Research Methods

These days, the vast majority of legal research is done using electronic re-sources. Legal publishers typically update them faster than they update print resources, and they allow for enhanced search capabilities in the form of full-text searching and hyperlinks providing instant access to related materials. In addition, electronic resources can be used anywhere there is an Internet con-nection, and there are many reliable sources of primary legal materials available at no cost. These free legal materials do not contain the enhancements available in commercial databases, but the core content is there. Secondary sources, on the other hand, are subject to copyright and priced at a premium.

Many researchers focus on the nuances of particular electronic platforms as the key to efficient and effective legal research. The appearance and func-tionality of these interfaces changes frequently, however, so sophisticated re-searchers need to dig deeper than a familiarity with a given platform as it is currently designed. Instead, the key to effective legal research is to understand and employ a variety of research methods. Every platform will support some combination of the research methods described below; if you are proficient with them, you will be successful with any platform you choose to use both now and in the future.

In the past, every sophisticated research method was *human ordered*. This means that legal material publishers and their attorney editors worked hard to structure their materials in thoughtful ways, and they created tools to ease the process of legal research by making connections between these materials. Examples of human ordered research methods include indexes, headnotes, tables of contents, subject headings, and statutory and regulatory annotations. Human ordered research methods were indispensable when legal materials were only available in a print format. Even now, the electronic versions of common legal materials remain rooted in their original print publication schemes. It drives their organization, layout, citation form, and sometimes even the timeline for the release of new content. As a result, human ordered research methods are still of enormous use.

In the digital age, additional research methods are available due to the advent of *machine recall*, or the use of a computer algorithm to retrieve and order results. The most popular research method of this type is natural language searching, but it also includes searching with fields or segments as well as the use of citing references retrieved by a citator like Shepard's or KeyCite.

Efficient and effective research hinges on your ability to pick and choose among different types of research methods, including both those that are human ordered and those that utilize machine recall. The research methods you choose will depend on the needs of a particular research assignment, and you should change the methods you employ based on the focus of a given assignment. Your quickest path to a research rut is to become a "one trick pony" and default to the same research method for every research project. Do not fall into this trap, as your end result will suffer for it.

Natural Language Searching

Made famous by Internet search engines like Google, natural language searching is very popular in today's legal research platforms, including Westlaw and Lexis Advance. Natural language searching is available in most of the low-cost legal research providers as well, such as Casemaker or Fastcase. Natural language searching looks for any word located anywhere in the selected content. Results are usually listed by relevance, but they can also be displayed by date, most cited, alphabetical order, or another means of ordering the results.

Natural language searching is a comfortable way to search because regular searching of web browsers is a part of most people's daily lives. Its greatest strength is its ability to find research results no matter what you input into the search box. This flexibility makes it a strong choice for "fishing expeditions" when you are researching in a new area or otherwise do not know where to start or the best vocabulary to use.

Natural language searching requires a great deal of deference to the search algorithm, however, as well as a strong aptitude in using search filters to narrow your results. It is not designed for comprehensive research, but it is an excellent option if you wish to find a helpful secondary source or one good primary law source to use to jump to additional relevant content.

Targeted Searching: Using Fields & Segments

Targeted searching using fields and segments is another research method utilizing machine recall, but it is much narrower and more precise than natural language searching. Westlaw calls this *field searching*, and Lexis Advance calls it *segment searching*, but they refer to the same search technique. This research method allows you to specify the exact portion of a type of legal document you wish to search. The search algorithm on whatever platform you are using will search those portions — ignoring every other part of the legal documents you chose. Note, also, that the fields or segments available will change based on the type of material you are researching. An important tip in using fields or segments effectively is that you must select a narrow set of materials you wish to use on Westlaw or Lexis Advance, such as "Pennsylvania State Cases," before selecting your field or segment. If you fail to do so, both platforms will only provide the bare minimum of field/segment options because they do not have enough information about the type of material you plan to use.

In case law research, for example, there are fields/segments that focus on a person, including the judge, an attorney involved in the case, or the name of a party to the case. If you wish to find every appellate-level case in Pennsylvania involving the Hershey Chocolate Co., as just one example, your use of the party name field/segment would look like this:

- advanced: TI("Hershey Chocolate Co.") (*using fields in Westlaw*)
- name("Hershey Chocolate Co.") (*using segments in Lexis Advance*)

In addition to the fields/segments of cases focusing on a person, you can also do field/segment searches for a number, such as the case citation or a docket number, and fields/segments focused on the substance of the case, including the synopsis/overview, the holding/outcome, or the headnotes. Keep in mind that these are just samples. There are many other fields/segments available for your use. You do not need to memorize the available fields or segments; they are readily available via the advanced search option on each platform.

Subject Indexes

Subject indexes are among the most valuable human ordered research methods. The connections are more thoughtful than a computer algorithm can achieve, so it is often easier to trust your results with human ordered tools.

For materials already organized by subject, such as a code (statutory or regulatory) or a multi-volume treatise set, an index allows you to pinpoint the most important sections for your research. This is true even if the content you need is dispersed throughout the set. Indexes were invaluable access points back when all legal research was done in print, but their speed and accuracy continue to provide great value to researchers who use electronic indexes in online databases. One of the strongest features of an index is that it is built to be very forgiving when it comes to vocabulary. Publishers and attorney editors create cross-references throughout an index to help steer you to the right place. For example, if you use the index to do statutory research in Pennsylvania and look up "water pollution," the index will direct you to "water quality" instead. Once you find something on point, be sure to leverage the organizational strengths of these subject-based compilations. Whether it is a statute, a regulation, or a section of a secondary source, make sure you use the table of contents to look for other helpful material nearby.

In case law research, where new decisions are only published chronologically, the closest equivalent to a subject index is the headnote system.[3] In this system, attorney-editors extract the major points of law from a case, summarize them in brief "headnotes," and then classify them by subject. It is done in much the same way we tag online content these days, but on a larger scale. If you can find a relevant tag within the classification system, you should find every case within a given jurisdiction with at least one major point of law on the same subject.[4]

An especially helpful use of indexing is using "subject headings" to search legal periodical indexes. Legal Source, the Index to Legal Periodicals, and Legal-Trac are all examples of legal periodical indexes. They contain a very large number of journal titles, which makes them your best bet for comprehensive research in legal periodicals, but they do not have full-text searching capabilities.

---

3. The headnote system is also referred to as the digest system and the Topic & Key Number system.

4. The headnote system is discussed in greater detail in Chapter 2, Judicial Opinions. All federal and state jurisdictions use the same classification system, so it is easy to jump between jurisdictions.

Instead, they search only select fields, such as title, author, and abstract. To improve the precision of this type of search, an editor applies a controlled set of subject headings (again, much like tags) to each article in the periodical index. These subject headings reflect the main focus of the article, so they allow you to run a search for articles based on their primary focus, rather than any time your search terms appear in any one of the available fields.

Overall, subject indexes are shortcuts designed and executed by human beings to help you get to relevant information as efficiently and effectively as you can. They are especially useful when you are drowning in too much information and need to narrow your results. Subject indexed materials can dramatically reduce the number of irrelevant results you receive, and they help with vocabulary issues as well as the challenges in pulling together relevant information when it treads across multiple subject areas or different jurisdictions.

Terms and Connectors Searching

Terms and connectors searching (or Boolean searching) is a hybrid approach that combines elements of both human ordered and machine recall techniques, and it is used very heavily by legal practitioners because it provides greater precision and control than any other research method. For example, it is the only research method that can do a comprehensive search for a precise list of each and every time a particular word or phrase occurs in a given set of legal materials. Also, terms and connectors searching is your strongest choice for trying to prove a negative, which means demonstrating with confidence that law does not exist on a given issue in your binding jurisdiction. Proving a negative is a routine occurrence in the practice of law. Terms and connectors searching is available on Westlaw, Lexis Advance, and Bloomberg Law, as well as on low-cost providers and many open access sources, with some minor variations from one provider to another.

Searching with terms and connectors is exactly what it sounds like — it is the creation and execution of a search string consisting of "terms" and "connectors." Terms are the words and phrases you select to express the legal concepts at issue in your research, and connectors are the operators you place between these words and phrases to relate them to one another. Note that there are basic connectors and proximity connectors, so you can control how closely related you want the words and phrases to be. For examples of widely used connectors, see Table 1-3.

In broad terms, these are the steps you should follow in drafting a terms and connectors search: (1) identify the components of your search; (2) brain-

Table 1-3. Selected Connectors and Illustrations

"AND"	This connector is used to retrieve documents that include all search terms in the list. For example, the search string **organic AND contamination AND pesticide** would yield documents containing all three words. Documents containing one or two words, but not the other, would not be retrieved.
"OR"	This command is used to retrieve documents that include any of the search terms in the list. For example, the command **physician OR surgeon** would yield documents containing either the word "physician," the word "surgeon," or both.
" "	Quotation marks around a set of words will retrieve documents that include the exact words within quotes. For example, a search for "weapons of mass destruction" would only yield documents containing this exact phrase.
NOT	The command "NOT" is used to exclude specific words from the documents retrieved. For example, the command **psychiatrist NOT psychologist** would retrieve documents containing the word "psychiatrist," but no documents containing the word "psychologist."
/s	The "/s" connector will retrieve documents where specified words are in the same sentence. For example, **hearsay /s statement** will retrieve "the defendant made a hearsay statement," "the statement was hearsay," and "the plaintiff objected to the statement on the grounds of hearsay." It will not retrieve documents where the words "hearsay" and "statement" are present, but in different sentences.
/p	The "/p" connector will retrieve documents where specified words are in the same paragraph. For example, **divorce /p insurance** will retrieve documents with "divorce" and "insurance" in the same paragraph. They may be in the same sentence or different sentences. It will not retrieve documents where the words "divorce" and "insurance" are present, but in different paragraphs.
/n	The "/n" connector will retrieve documents within a specified number of words. Note that "n" is only a placeholder for the number you choose. For example, **written /4 contract** will retrieve "written contract" and "a contract she had written by hand." It will not retrieve documents where the words "written" and "contract" are present, but more than four words apart.

storm key terms for each search component, including synonyms, related concepts, and word variations; (3) determine how you wish to relate your search components to one another; and (4) select the appropriate connectors and place them within your search string.[5] After carefully planning your terms and connectors search in this manner, run the search and then thoughtfully assess your results.

Keep in mind that when using terms and connectors, the search algorithm finds *exactly* what you requested in your chosen set of materials. Unlike a natural language search, terms and connectors searching is terribly unforgiving if you make any spelling errors, and you can often tell right away if your search is poorly drafted because it will retrieve either too many or too few results. If you take the time to carefully consider what happened, you will be in a much better position to adapt your search so it works better when you rerun it. With continued planning and additional practice, terms and connectors searching will get much easier, and you will ultimately reach a point where these searches will be one of the most efficient and effective tools in your research arsenal.

V. Organizing and Managing Your Research

As you go through the steps in your research process for a given project, you should record and organize your findings. It will help keep your research under control, especially if you have multiple open research projects. Keep track of where you searched, what research method and/or search terms you used, how well it worked, and anything new you learned. You can track this information using online tools, including the "folders" for storing and annotating documents on both Westlaw and Lexis Advance, or using pen and paper. Use whatever works best for you.

Be thoughtful throughout your research project, and do not hesitate to return to your preliminary analysis if your research is not as fruitful as you expected. If you are researching multiple issues together, consider researching each issue separately. This minimizes the chance of confusion, and it narrows the results you need to review. If you need to learn more about the legal jargon in an area and possible terms of art, revert to a secondary source. You can also try a different research platform and/or different research methods, as the relevant information may not be located where you guessed it would be.

The final step in a research project is delivering the finished product to the requestor. Possibilities range from formal delivery of your work, such as a

---

5. For more information on drafting a terms and connectors search, including walking you through a sample search, see Catherine M. Dunn, *Use Terms and Connectors for Precise Search Results*, ABA STUDENT LAWYER, Apr./May 2015, at 21–22.

written research memo or research results embedded into a court pleading, to less formal options, such as an outline for an oral discussion of the project. At the outset of your research project, make sure you know exactly how the person assigning the project wishes to see your final results.

Chapter 2

Judicial Opinions

Written opinions explaining a court's resolution of the issues in a particular case are a form of primary authority. In some situations, judicial opinions will be the source of the rule of law that controls an issue. In other situations, the controlling rule will be a statutory provision or an administrative rule that has been interpreted or explained by a court. Either way, the number of judicial opinions written each year is vast; knowing how to locate judicial opinions efficiently is a critical research skill.

This chapter begins with a general introduction to the state and federal courts in Pennsylvania because the court that decided a case affects where you will find the case, how you will cite it, and how much weight it will have in your analysis. The chapter then discusses typical features of reported cases, and describes a variety of methods for locating them. The chapter concludes with an overview of case analysis.

I. State and Federal Courts

The basic court structure in most jurisdictions includes trial courts, intermediate courts of appeals, and a court of last resort, often called the "supreme" court. These courts exist in both the state and federal systems.

A. Pennsylvania State Courts[1]

The Pennsylvania Constitution of 1968 organized the judiciary into the Unified Judicial System, which consists of the Supreme, Superior and Common-

---

1. The website for the Pennsylvania judiciary, www.pacourts.us, contains a history of Pennsylvania's courts, an explanation of their jurisdiction, and links to court websites.

Figure 2-1. Pennsylvania Unified Judicial System

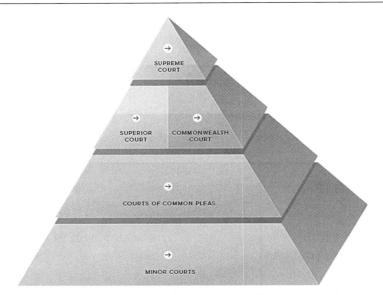

Source: Website for the Unified Judicial System of Pennsylvania at http://www.pacourts.us/learn.

wealth Courts, Courts of Common Pleas, and various special or minor courts.[2] Pennsylvania's Unified Judicial System is illustrated in Figure 2-1.

The Supreme Court of Pennsylvania is the highest court in the state. It hears appeals from the Commonwealth and Superior Courts. With the exception of capital (death penalty) cases, which the court is required to hear, the court has discretion to choose the issues it will resolve. The Supreme Court of Pennsylvania is composed of seven justices, who sit *en banc*[3] to hear cases. The court's decisions are binding on all state courts in Pennsylvania.

The Commonwealth Court of Pennsylvania and the Superior Court of Pennsylvania are the intermediate appellate courts. Their decisions are binding on

---

2. These minor courts include the Philadelphia Municipal Court, Pittsburgh Magistrates Court, Philadelphia Traffic Court, and Magisterial District Courts. The minor courts hear less serious, non-jury criminal and civil cases, and all traffic cases. In some minor courts, the judges who preside are not required to have a law degree.

3. *En banc* generally refers to the full court hearing a case. *See Black's Law Dictionary* (Bryan A. Garner ed., 10th ed., Thomson West 2014). In Pennsylvania, court procedures establish that seven judges constitute an *en banc* panel for the Commonwealth Court, and nine for the Superior Court, even though there are more judges on both courts.

trial courts all over the state. The Commonwealth Court has jurisdiction over appeals involving Pennsylvania's government or its agencies. The court hears all cases involving the Commonwealth of Pennsylvania as a plaintiff or defendant, election cases, real estate tax appeals, and eminent domain cases. It can also hear zoning cases. Cases are normally heard by three-judge *panels*; occasionally, an *en banc* panel of seven judges will be assigned to hear certain cases, and some cases are resolved by a single judge. The Superior Court hears criminal appeals and civil appeals that do not fall within the jurisdiction of the Commonwealth Court. The Superior Court sits in three-judge panels to hear most cases. Occasionally, the Superior Court will specially order consideration of a case by an *en banc* panel of nine judges.

The Courts of Common Pleas are the trial courts in Pennsylvania. At least one of these courts exists in each of Pennsylvania's sixty judicial districts. Trial court decisions from one district are not binding on courts in any other districts, but can be persuasive in the absence of decisions from a higher court.

B. Federal Courts[4]

The highest court in the federal system is the United States Supreme Court. Its decisions on issues of federal law are binding on state and federal courts nationwide. The Court does not have the final say on matters of purely state law, however; that authority rests with the highest court of each state. The Court grants only a small percentage of the requests for review that are filed each year, so for practical purposes the intermediate appellate courts are the courts of last resort for most litigants.

The intermediate appellate courts in the federal system are called United States Circuit Courts of Appeals, and are organized into thirteen circuits. Eleven of the federal circuits are based on geography. Pennsylvania is in the Third Circuit, which also encompasses Delaware and New Jersey. The decisions of a circuit court are binding only on the trial courts within the same circuit; trial courts do not have to follow appellate decisions from other circuits. If two or more circuit courts reach different conclusions on the same legal issue, the difference will stand unless the Supreme Court addresses the issue.

---

4. The website for the federal judiciary, www.uscourts.gov, contains explanations of jurisdiction and other helpful information, including a map showing the federal circuits.

The remaining two circuit courts are the District of Columbia Circuit and the Federal Circuit. The District of Columbia Circuit is the smallest in terms of its geographic coverage, but is influential because it reviews a significant number of federal agency decisions. The Federal Circuit has exclusive appellate jurisdiction over patent law cases and cases arising under certain federal statutes, regardless of where the case originated.

Federal trial courts are called United States District Courts and represent subdivisions within each federal circuit. Every state has at least one district court, and many states have more than one district court. Pennsylvania is subdivided into three districts: eastern (Philadelphia), middle (Harrisburg and Scranton), and western (Pittsburgh). Delaware has one federal district court; New Jersey has a single district court, but the court is internally organized into three divisions covering different areas of the state. As in the state system, decisions of one district court are not binding on another district court, even within the same circuit, but can be cited as persuasive authority.

C. Courts of Other States

Most states have a three-tier court system like Pennsylvania and the federal judiciary. A few states, such as Maine and New Hampshire, do not have an intermediate appellate court. In some states, the highest court is not called a "supreme" court; in New York, the highest court is the Court of Appeals, and in Massachusetts and Maine, the highest court is the Supreme Judicial Court. If you are researching the law of another state for the first time, take a moment to look for the website of that state's judiciary and familiarize yourself with the court hierarchy there.

II. Reporters

Judicial opinions are published chronologically in volumes called *reporters*. In the pre-digital era, reporters were the only source of opinions other than the courts themselves. Some courts published all or most of their opinions; some were more selective. Only the cases that were released for publication in official reporters were regarded as having precedential value. Different jurisdictions developed their own rules for when litigants could cite to opinions that had not been released for publication. These variations continue to have practical consequences for researchers today.

One consequence is that, in most jurisdictions—including Pennsylvania—"published" opinions are still cited to the reporter or reporters in which they appear, regardless of how and where they are located during the research process. Another consequence is that, even though many "unpublished" opinions are now readily available online, court rules in some jurisdictions still limit how and when those opinions can be used. In Pennsylvania, the Supreme Court publishes all of its opinions, but the appellate courts publish only a small percentage of their opinions. An unpublished opinion cannot be cited or relied on in the Superior Court except in very narrow circumstances.[5] However, in the Commonwealth Court, unpublished opinions written after 2008 can be cited as persuasive authority.[6] In federal courts, including those seated in Pennsylvania, unpublished opinions can be cited as persuasive authority.[7]

A. General Features of Reporters

The volumes of a reporter are typically numbered in sequence, so citing a reported case requires both a volume number and a page number. In addition, most reporters have been published in more than one series, so the names (and abbreviations) of reporters often incorporate an ordinal number. The first series of *Atlantic Reporter* (abbreviated "A."), which includes cases from Pennsylvania appellate courts, was published from 1895 to 1938. In 1939, the first volume of *Atlantic Reporter, Second Series* ("A.2d") was published. The current series, *Atlantic Reporter, Third Series* ("A.3d"), began in 2010.

It is important to note the series, not just the reporter volume, when locating and citing published opinions. The case reported at page 286 of volume 34 of *Atlantic Reporter, Third Series* (34 A.3d 286) is a decision of the Pennsylvania Commonwealth Court in a 2011 appeal from a zoning decision; the case reported at page 286 of volume 34 of *Atlantic Reporter, Second Series* (34 A.2d 286) is a decision in a 1943 divorce suit.

To make cases available before the bound reporter volumes can be published, publishers often supply subscribers with paperback *advance sheets*. The advance sheets use the same pagination that will eventually be used in the hardbound volumes. Thus, as soon as a case is assigned a page number in the advance sheets, it can be cited to the appropriate reporter series.

---

5. *See* 210 Pa. Code § 65.37, Unpublished Memoranda Decisions. Section 65.37 allows a party to request that an unpublished opinion of the Superior Court be released for publication, but this is at the court's sole discretion.

6. *See* 210 Pa. Code § 69.414, Citing Judicial Opinions in Filings.

7. Federal Rule of Appellate Procedure 32.1 has allowed this practice since 2007; before then, litigants had to check internal rules and operating procedures for the court in which they were appearing to see whether that court allowed citation of unpublished opinions.

Online sources of judicial opinions typically provide the volume and page number—when available—of the reporter or reporters where the opinions are published. When you retrieve a published opinion on Westlaw, Lexis Advance, or Bloomberg Law, you will be able to see where that opinion is published and cite it as though you had retrieved it from a reporter. Other online sources provide that information as well, but are not always updated as quickly for very recent decisions.

1. Types of Reporters

Some reporters are specific to a single court. Others publish cases from the courts of a particular state or region. In addition to these state and regional reporters, which are the most widely used in practice, reporters can be devoted to a particular area of the law, such as bankruptcy or procedure.

Another variation is that some reporters are "official," while others are "unofficial." Official reporters are approved or published by a branch of government within a particular jurisdiction and often lack editorial content. Court rules typically require citation to the official reporter of a jurisdiction. Unofficial reporters are produced commercially and often add editorial content to the cases. There is some overlap between the two types of reporters, however. Pennsylvania is an example of a jurisdiction where a private publisher currently publishes the official reporter under agreement with the state.

2. Editorial Enhancements in Reported Cases

A reported case contains the full text of the court's opinion. If concurring or dissenting opinions were filed, they will be included also. In addition to the text, publishers add information, or "editorial enhancements," designed to help researchers understand the case and find similar cases. These editorial enhancements are not part of the decision itself and should never be cited as authority. The case excerpt in Figure 2-2 provides an example from *Pennsylvania State Reports*, a West reporter. Figure 2-3 is the same case illustrated in Figure 2-2, but shows how that case appears on Westlaw.

Some editorial enhancements are simply descriptive information about the parties and the case. The parties are listed with their procedural designations, such as appellant/appellee or petitioner/respondent. The name of the judge who authored the opinion generally precedes the opinion; the designation "per curiam," or "by the court," means no single judge is credited with authorship of the opinion. Sometimes attorneys are listed. Some reporters provide *parallel citations* to the same case in other reporters.

Figure 2-2. Excerpt from *Mason-Dixon Resorts, L.P. v. Pennsylvania Gaming Control Bd.*, 52 A.3d 1087 (Pa. 2012)

MASON–DIXON RESORTS v. GAMING CONTROL BD.   Pa. **1087**
Cite as 52 A.3d 1087 (Pa. 2012)

Names of parties with their procedural designations ⎯⎯

**MASON–DIXON RESORTS,
L.P., Appellant**

v.

**PENNSYLVANIA GAMING CONTROL
BOARD, Appellee**

v.

Woodlands Fayette, LLC, Intervenor.

Name of Court ⟶ Supreme Court of Pennsylvania.

Dates ⎯⎯ Argued March 7, 2012.
Decided Aug. 20, 2012.

Synopsis ⟶ **Background:** Disappointed applicant for Category 3 slot machine license sought review of order and adjudication of the Pennsylvania Gaming Control Board. Successful applicant intervened.

Holdings: The Supreme Court, No. 54 WM 2011, Castille, C.J., held that:

(1) successful applicant's gaming facility was located "in a well-established resort hotel" within meaning of statute;

(2) successful applicant satisfied eligibility requirement that it have 275 guest rooms under common ownership;

(3) disappointed applicant failed to establish due process violation;

(4) question of how to weigh statutory factors was for the Board;

(5) Board acted prudently in determining that successful applicant was financially suitable; and

Result ⎯ (6) evidence supported finding that successful applicant had suitable character.

Notation of any concurring or dissenting opinions ⟶ Affirmed.

Saylor, J., joined in part and concurred in result in part.

Baer, J., concurred in part, dissented in part, and filed opinion, in which Todd, J., joined.

Headnotes identified by West topic and key number, and numbered to correspond to their source in the text ⟶ **1. Gaming** ⟜4

With regard to an error of law, Supreme Court's review of a decision of the Pennsylvania Gaming Control Board is de novo, and its scope of review is plenary. 4 Pa.C.S.A. § 1204.

2. Gaming ⟜4

In reviewing decision of the Pennsylvania Gaming Control Board, Supreme Court must affirm unless it finds that the Board committed an error of law, or acted arbitrarily and with a capricious disregard of the evidence; the Supreme Court may not simply substitute its judgment for the discretionary decision-making authority of the Board. 4 Pa.C.S.A. § 1204.

3. Gaming ⟜4

Gaming facility located in an existing structure on resort grounds, about 1.2 miles from the primary hotel complex, was located "in a well-established resort hotel" within meaning of statute governing eligibility for Category 3 slot machine licenses; "hotel" was expansively defined by statute as "a building or buildings in which members of the public may, for a consideration, obtain sleeping accommodations." 4 Pa. C.S.A. §§ 1103, 1305(a).

See publication Words and Phrases for other judicial constructions and definitions.

4. Gaming ⟜4

Applicant seeking Category 3 slot machine license satisfied eligibility requirement that it have 275 guest rooms under common ownership at the time of its application; although documentary proof of lodging ownership submitted by applicant could have been more succinct and precise, any of the varying numbers of rooms claimed to be owned by applicant exceeded the 275 statutory minimum, and there was no proof to contradict claim that the rooms were "all owned 100%" by applicant. 4 Pa.C.S.A. § 1305.

5. Gaming ⟜4

Regulations adopted by Pennsylvania Gaming Control Board, requiring timely,

Source: *Atlantic Reporter, Third Series*. Reprinted with permission of Thomson/West.

Figure 2-2. (continued). Excerpt from *Mason-Dixon Resorts, L.P. v. Pennsylvania Gaming Control Bd.*, 52 A.3d 1087 (Pa. 2012)

1088 Pa.   52 ATLANTIC REPORTER, 3d SERIES

Examples of cross-references to statutory and constitutional provisions

specific objections during the Board's hearing process, were reasonable. 1 Pa. Code § 35.126(b); 58 Pa.Code §§ 441a.7(t), 494a.1(c), 494a.2, 494a.7(a).

6. Gaming ☞4

Disappointed applicant for Category 3 slot machine license waived claim that it was denied due process and was prejudiced because of a political contribution made by a competing applicant's principal to Board member who was previously a member of the State House, where disappointed applicant did not raise any objection to the Board member's participation in the licensing decision. U.S.C.A. Const. Amend. 14; 4 Pa.C.S.A. § 1305.

7. Constitutional Law ☞4285
Gaming ☞4

Disappointed applicant for Category 3 slot machine license failed to establish a due process violation based on Pennsylvania Gaming Control Board's failure to reopen the record so applicant could introduce newly discovered financial information about competing applicant; although Board denied the petition to reopen the record, Board nevertheless forwarded the additional materials and argument regarding competitor's finances to its financial investigations unit, which produced an addendum report for the Board in advance of the Board's final decision. U.S.C.A. Const. Amend. 14; 4 Pa.C.S.A. § 1305.

8. Constitutional Law ☞4285
Gaming ☞4

Disappointed applicant for Category 3 slot machine license failed to establish a due process violation based on post-decision release of a grand jury report broadly criticizing the inception and early operations of the Pennsylvania Gaming Control Board; nothing in the report specifically impugned the proceedings at issue, and Board filed a memorandum explaining its decision to reject disappointed applicant's

claims based on the grand jury report. U.S.C.A. Const.Amend. 14; 4 Pa.C.S.A. § 1305.

9. Gaming ☞4

In considering applications for Category 3 slot machine license, Pennsylvania Gaming Control Board was authorized to use a closed executive session to receive certain confidential information which applicants were required to submit. 4 Pa. C.S.A. §§ 1206(f), 1305; 65 Pa.C.S.A. § 708(a)(5).

10. Constitutional Law ☞4285
Gaming ☞4

Disappointed applicant for Category 3 slot machine license failed to establish a due process violation based on negative public statements by the then-Governor about the location of applicant's proposed gaming facility; Governor was no less entitled to an opinion on siting gaming facilities than other citizens, there was no evidence that public statements by the Governor or any elected official had any undue influence on the licensing decision at issue, and there was no allegation of improper ex parte communications on the matter. U.S.C.A. Const.Amend. 14; 4 Pa. C.S.A. § 1305.

11. Gaming ☞4

Members of Pennsylvania Gaming Control Board considering award of Category 3 slot machine license were free to make unannounced visits to the locations and facilities advocated by the applicants, which were operational and open to the public. 4 Pa.C.S.A. § 1305.

12. Constitutional Law ☞4285
Gaming ☞4

Disappointed applicant for Category 3 slot machine license failed to establish a due process violation based on Pennsylvania Gaming Control Board's allegedly improper consideration of negative public

Figure 2-2. (continued). Excerpt from *Mason-Dixon Resorts, L.P. v. Pennsylvania Gaming Control Bd.*, 52 A.3d 1087 (Pa. 2012)

MASON–DIXON RESORTS v. GAMING CONTROL BD.   Pa.   **1089**
Cite as 52 A.3d 1087 (Pa. 2012)

commentary about its proposed location; Board was authorized to receive and consider public input about slot machine license applicants, and there was no prohibition on the submission of petitions in support or opposition to a proposed gaming facility. U.S.C.A. Const.Amend. 14; 4 Pa.C.S.A. §§ 1205, 1305.

13. Gaming ⚖4

Question of how to weigh statutory factors was for the Pennsylvania Gaming Control Board considering applications for Category 3 slot machine license. 4 Pa. C.S.A. §§ 1305, 1325.

14. Gaming ⚖4

Supreme Court reviewing Pennsylvania Gaming Control Board's award of Category 3 slot machine license was not authorized to employ its own discretion in determining which applicant was the best applicant, and was not empowered to sift through the voluminous evidence, reweighing it; the Court's review was to determine whether the Board acted arbitrarily or in capricious disregard of the evidence when it considered the relevant factors.

15. Gaming ⚖4

The "prudent man" rule governs the Pennsylvania Gaming Control Board's conduct in determining financial suitability of a slots license applicant. 4 Pa.C.S.A. § 1201(h.2); 20 Pa.C.S.A. § 7302(b).

16. Gaming ⚖4

Pennsylvania Gaming Control Board, considering applications for Category 3 slot machine license, acted prudently in determining that successful applicant was financially suitable for slots gaming licensure; although successful applicant projected the lowest gaming revenue of all applications, Board weighed that evidence in the context of the new "non-cannibalized" revenue potential from successful applicant's extensive out-of-state clientele, and Board concluded that any alleged financial instability of another property owned by the same trust that owned successful applicant would not undermine the financial suitability of the proposed gaming facility. 4 Pa.C.S.A. §§ 1206(f), 1305; 65 Pa.C.S.A. § 708(a)(5).

17. Gaming ⚖4

The purpose of requirement that a slots license applicant establish "suitability, including good character, honesty and integrity," is to support the General Assembly's special concern that gaming in the Commonwealth not be perceived as corrupt. 4 Pa.C.S.A. § 1310(a)(1).

18. Gaming ⚖4

Evidence supported finding of Pennsylvania Gaming Control Board that successful applicant for Category 3 slot machine license satisfied requirement that an applicant establish suitability, including good character, honesty and integrity; although there were allegations of wrongdoing by a principal of successful applicant, all records of the alleged incident were expunged, no criminal prosecution was pursued and no conviction resulted, and the Board was satisfied with explanations provided, and the timeline of relevant events. 4 Pa.C.S.A. §§ 1305, 1310(a)(1).

Stephen David Schrier, Blank Rome LLP, Philadelphia, for Mason–Dixon Resorts, L.P.

David Cornelius Hittinger Jr., Linda S. Lloyd, Cyrus Raphael Pitre, Richard Douglas Sherman, for Pennsylvania Gaming Control Board.

Adrian Renz King Jr., Raymond Adam Quaglia, Ballard Spahr Andrews & Ingersoll, L.L.P., Philadelphia, Tami Bogutz

Attorneys

Figure 2-2. (continued). Excerpt from *Mason-Dixon Resorts, L.P. v. Pennsylvania Gaming Control Bd.*, 52 A.3d 1087 (Pa. 2012)

1090 Pa.   52 ATLANTIC REPORTER, 3d SERIES

Judges who participated in the decision ——→

Opinion of the court: anything preceding this point should not be cited or quoted

Author of the majority opinion

Steinberg, Flaster/Greenberg, P.C. Cherry Hill, NJ, for Woodlands Fayette, LLC.

CASTILLE, C.J., SAYLOR, EAKIN, BAER, TODD, McCAFFERY, ORIE MELVIN, JJ.

OPINION

Chief Justice CASTILLE.

This is a direct appeal filed by Mason–Dixon Resorts, L.P. ("appellant"), from the decision of the Pennsylvania Gaming Control Board (the "Board") which awarded a Category 3 slot machine license to Intervenor Woodlands Fayette, L.L.C. ("Woodlands"). We affirm.

Background

In July 2004, the General Assembly enacted the Pennsylvania Race Horse Development and Gaming Act (the "Act"), 4 Pa.C.S. §§ 1101–1904. The Act provides, *inter alia*, a statutory framework for legalized slot machine gaming at a limited number of licensed facilities throughout the Commonwealth. "Three categories of slot machine gaming facilities are authorized under the Act. 4 Pa.C.S. § 1301. A Category 1 license authorizes the placement and operation of slot machines at existing horse racing tracks; a Category 2 license authorizes the placement and operation of slot machines in standalone facilities; and a Category 3 license authorizes the placement and operation of slot machines in resort hotels. 4 Pa.C.S. §§ 1302–1305." *Station Square Gaming L.P. v. Pa. Gaming Control Bd.*, 592 Pa. 664, 927 A.2d 232, 236 (2007) ("*Station Square* ").

The criteria for the award of a Category 3 slot machine license are set forth in Section 1305 of the Act. Specifically at issue here are the requirements of Section 1305(a)(1):

(a) Eligibility.—

(1) A person may be eligible to apply for a Category 3 slot machine license if the

applicant, its affiliate, intermediary, subsidiary or holding company has not applied for or been approved or issued a Category 1 or Category 2 slot machine license and the person is seeking to locate a Category 3 licensed facility in a well-established resort hotel having no fewer than 275 guest rooms under common ownership and having substantial year-round recreational guest amenities. The applicant for a Category 3 license shall be the owner or be a wholly owned subsidiary of the owner of the well-established resort hotel....

4 Pa.C.S. § 1305(a)(1). To qualify as a "well-established resort hotel with substantial year-round recreational guest amenities," the facility must offer "a complement of amenities characteristic of a well-established resort hotel, including but not limited to" the following:

(1) Sports and recreational activities and facilities such as a golf course or golf driving range.
(2) Tennis courts.
(3) Swimming pools or a water park.
(4) A health spa.
(5) Meeting and banquet facilities.
(6) Entertainment facilities.
(7) Restaurant facilities.
(8) Downhill or cross-country skiing facilities.
(9) Bowling lanes.
(10) Movie theaters.

58 Pa.Code § 441a.23(a). Additional criteria for the Board's consideration in granting a slot machine license are listed in the Act, including: restrictions regarding the good character of applicants, and requiring letters of reference from law enforcement entities (4 Pa.C.S. § 1310); business restrictions on who may own, control or hold key positions for a licensed facility (4 Pa. C.S. § 1311); and strict financial fitness requirements to ensure operational viability of the proposed facility (4 Pa.C.S. § 1313).

In addition to the other eligibility requirements of the Act, the Board "may also take into account the following factors

Figure 2-3. Excerpt from Westlaw version of *Mason-Dixon Resorts, L.P. v. Pennsylvania Gaming Control Bd.*, 617 Pa. 18, 52 A.3d 1087 (Pa. 2012)

Mason-Dixon Resorts, L.P. v. Pennsylvania Gaming Control Bd., 617 Pa. 18 (2012)

52 A.3d 1087

If a case is published in more than one West reporter, the Westlaw version will always provide parallel cites

617 Pa. 18

Supreme Court of Pennsylvania.

MASON–DIXON RESORTS, L.P., Appellant

v.

PENNSYLVANIA GAMING
CONTROL BOARD, Appellee

v.

Woodlands Fayette, LLC, Intervenor.

Argued March 7, 2012.
|
Decided Aug. 20, 2012.

Synopsis
Background: Disappointed applicant for Category 3 slot machine license sought review of order and adjudication of the Pennsylvania Gaming Control Board. Successful applicant intervened.

Holdings: The Supreme Court, No. 54 WM 2011, Castille, C.J., held that:

[1] successful applicant's gaming facility was located "in a well-established resort hotel" within meaning of statute;

[2] successful applicant satisfied eligibility requirement that it have 275 guest rooms under common ownership;

[3] disappointed applicant failed to establish due process violation;

[4] question of how to weigh statutory factors was for the Board;

[5] Board acted prudently in determining that successful applicant was financially suitable; and

[6] evidence supported finding that successful applicant had suitable character.

Affirmed.

Saylor, J., joined in part and concurred in result in part.

Baer, J., concurred in part, dissented in part, and filed opinion, in which Todd, J., joined.

West Headnotes (18)

[1]   **Gaming and Lotteries**
      Judicial review in general
With regard to an error of law, Supreme Court's review of a decision of the Pennsylvania Gaming Control Board is de novo, and its scope of review is plenary. 4 Pa.C.S.A. § 1204.

Cases that cite this headnote

[2]   **Gaming and Lotteries**
      Judicial review in general
In reviewing decision of the Pennsylvania Gaming Control Board, Supreme Court must affirm unless it finds that the Board committed an error of law, or acted arbitrarily and with a capricious disregard of the evidence; the Supreme Court may not simply substitute its judgment for the discretionary decision-making authority of the Board. 4 Pa.C.S.A. § 1204.

Cases that cite this headnote

[3]   **Gaming and Lotteries**
      Casinos and Gaming Establishments
Gaming facility located in an existing structure on resort grounds, about 1.2 miles from the primary hotel complex, was located "in a well-established resort hotel" within meaning of statute governing eligibility for Category 3 slot machine licenses; "hotel" was expansively defined by statute as "a building or buildings in which members

Headnotes are identified online by topic and subtopic, with a Key Number symbol; they are also linked to their source in the text

Link to the West Headnote system for finding similar cases

On Westlaw, cross-references are hyperlinked

[Pages 2 and 3 of this excerpt have been omitted]

Reprinted with permission of Thomson Reuters.

Figure 2-3. (continued). Excerpt from Westlaw version of *Mason-Dixon Resorts, L.P. v. Pennsylvania Gaming Control Bd.*, 617 Pa. 18, 52 A.3d 1087 (Pa. 2012)

Mason-Dixon Resorts, L.P. v. Pennsylvania Gaming Control Bd., 617 Pa. 18 (2012)

52 A.3d 1087

the Court's review was to determine whether the Board acted arbitrarily or in capricious disregard of the evidence when it considered the relevant factors.

1 Cases that cite this headnote

[15]   Gaming and Lotteries
     Casinos and Gaming Establishments

The "prudent man" rule governs the Pennsylvania Gaming Control Board's conduct in determining financial suitability of a slots license applicant. 4 Pa.C.S.A. § 1201(h.2); 20 Pa.C.S.A. § 7302(b).

Cases that cite this headnote

[16]   Gaming and Lotteries
     Casinos and Gaming Establishments

Pennsylvania Gaming Control Board, considering applications for Category 3 slot machine license, acted prudently in determining that successful applicant was financially suitable for slots gaming licensure; although successful applicant projected the lowest gaming revenue of all applications, Board weighed that evidence in the context of the new "non-cannibalized" revenue potential from successful applicant's extensive out-of-state clientele, and Board concluded that any alleged financial instability of another property owned by the same trust that owned successful applicant would not undermine the financial suitability of the proposed gaming facility. 4 Pa.C.S.A. §§ 1206(f), 1305; 65 Pa.C.S.A. § 708(a)(5).

Cases that cite this headnote

[17]   Gaming and Lotteries
     Casinos and Gaming Establishments

The purpose of requirement that a slots license applicant establish "suitability, including good character, honesty and integrity," is to support the General Assembly's special concern that gaming in the Commonwealth not be perceived as corrupt. 4 Pa.C.S.A. § 1310(a)(1).

Cases that cite this headnote

[18]   Gaming and Lotteries
     Personnel issues

Evidence supported finding of Pennsylvania Gaming Control Board that successful applicant for Category 3 slot machine license satisfied requirement that an applicant establish suitability, including good character, honesty and integrity; although there were allegations of wrongdoing by a principal of successful applicant, all records of the alleged incident were expunged, no criminal prosecution was pursued and no conviction resulted, and the Board was satisfied with explanations provided, and the timeline of relevant events. 4 Pa.C.S.A. §§ 1305, 1310(a)(1).

Cases that cite this headnote

Attorneys and Law Firms

**1089 Stephen David Schrier, Blank Rome LLP, Philadelphia, for Mason–Dixon Resorts, L.P.

David Cornelius Hittinger Jr., Linda S. Lloyd, Cyrus Raphael Pitre, Richard Douglas Sherman, for Pennsylvania Gaming Control Board.

Adrian Renz King Jr., Raymond Adam Quaglia, Ballard Spahr Andrews & Ingersoll, L.L.P., Philadelphia, ****1090** Tami Bogutz Steinberg, Flaster/Greenberg, P.C. Cherry Hill, NJ, for Woodlands Fayette, LLC.

The online version provides "star paging" for both reporters where this case appears; this is a pinpoint page reference to the *Atlantic Reporter*

Figure 2-3. (continued). Excerpt from Westlaw version of *Mason-Dixon Resorts, L.P. v. Pennsylvania Gaming Control Bd.*, 617 Pa. 18, 52 A.3d 1087 (Pa. 2012)

Mason-Dixon Resorts, L.P. v. Pennsylvania Gaming Control Bd., 617 Pa. 18 (2012)

52 A.3d 1087

Michael D. Sklar, John M. Donnelly, Levine, Staller, Sklar, Chan, Brown & Donnelly, Atlantic City, NJ, for Penn Harris Gaming.

Maria J. Jones, Fox Rothschild, L.L.P., Atlantic City, NJ, for Bushkill Group, Inc.

CASTILLE, C.J., SAYLOR, EAKIN, BAER, TODD, McCAFFERY, ORIE MELVIN, JJ.

OPINION

Chief Justice CASTILLE.

*24 This is a direct appeal filed by Mason–Dixon Resorts, L.P. ("appellant"), from the decision of the Pennsylvania Gaming Control Board (the "Board") which awarded a Category 3 slot machine license to Intervenor Woodlands Fayette, L.L.C. ("Woodlands"). We affirm.

Background

In July 2004, the General Assembly enacted the Pennsylvania Race Horse Development and Gaming Act (the "Act"), 4 Pa.C.S. §§ 1101–1904. The Act provides, *inter alia,* a statutory framework for legalized slot machine gaming at a limited number of licensed facilities throughout the Commonwealth. "Three categories of slot machine gaming facilities are authorized under the Act. 4 Pa.C.S. § 1301. A Category 1 license authorizes the placement and operation of slot machines at existing horse racing tracks; a Category 2 license authorizes the placement and operation of slot machines in standalone facilities; and a Category 3 license authorizes the placement and operation of slot machines in resort hotels. 4 Pa.C.S. §§ 1302–1305." *Station Square Gaming L.P. v. Pa. Gaming Control Bd.,* 592 Pa. 664, 927 A.2d 232, 236 (2007) ("*Station Square* ").

The criteria for the award of a Category 3 slot machine license are set forth in Section 1305 of the Act. Specifically at issue here are the requirements of Section 1305(a)(1):

(a) Eligibility.—

(1) A person may be eligible to apply for a Category 3 slot machine license if the applicant, its affiliate, intermediary, subsidiary or holding company has not applied for or been approved or issued a Category 1 or Category 2 slot machine license and the person is seeking to locate a Category 3 licensed facility in a well-established resort hotel having no fewer than 275 guest rooms under common ownership and having substantial year-round recreational guest amenities. The applicant for a Category 3 license shall be the owner or ***25** be a wholly owned subsidiary of the owner of the well-established resort hotel....

4 Pa.C.S. § 1305(a)(1). To qualify as a "well-established resort hotel with substantial year-round recreational guest amenities," the facility must offer "a complement of amenities characteristic of a well-established resort hotel, including but not limited to" the following:

(1) Sports and recreational activities and facilities such as a golf course or golf driving range.

(2) Tennis courts.

(3) Swimming pools or a water park.

(4) A health spa.

(5) Meeting and banquet facilities.

(6) Entertainment facilities.

(7) Restaurant facilities.

(8) Downhill or cross-country skiing facilities.

(9) Bowling lanes.

(10) Movie theaters.

58 Pa.Code § 441a.23(a). Additional criteria for the Board's consideration in granting a slot machine license are listed in the Act, including: restrictions regarding the good character of applicants, and requiring letters of reference from law enforcement entities (4 Pa.C.S. § 1310); business restrictions on who may own, control or hold key positions for a licensed facility (4 Pa.C.S. § 1311); and strict financial fitness requirements to ensure operational viability of the proposed facility (4 Pa.C.S. § 1313).

Star paging for *Pennsylvania State Reports*

Often a *synopsis*, or short summary, precedes the text of the opinion. The synopsis is not part of the opinion, but is a helpful tool for identifying helpful cases in a search result.

For research purposes, the most important editorial enhancements are the *headnotes*. A headnote summarizes a single point of law from an opinion. Most cases will have several headnotes; some only have one or two. Because headnotes are created by the publisher, the number of headnotes and their content will be different if the same case is published in different reporters.

Headnotes are numbered in sequence, and those numbers are repeated in the text of the opinion at the point in the text corresponding to the headnotes. Always go to the point in the text that supports the headnote and quote or cite that language instead of quoting or citing the headnote directly. The language in the headnote may closely resemble the language in the text of the opinion, but you cannot assume they are identical; even when the headnote and text are identical, only the text itself can be cited.

In addition to the sequential numbering, each headnote is assigned a specific topic and subtopic. These topics and subtopics vary depending on the publisher. As discussed in the next section, the topics and subtopics are part of an indexing system that allows researchers to find cases addressing similar topics.

The platform used for retrieving cases online will determine whether these editorial enhancements appear in the search result. Westlaw and Lexis Advance provide the most extensive editorial enhancements; Bloomberg Law provides more limited enhancements. Other platforms are typically limited to providing descriptive information, but without a separate synopsis or headnotes. In Pennsylvania, the headnotes of a case retrieved on Westlaw will be identical to the headnotes in a print reporter, because the reporters are West publications; the headnotes will be different if the case is retrieved on Lexis Advance.

3. Topical Indexes: Headnotes, Digests, and Key Numbers

Topical indexing systems are essential for finding cases in reporters. In print, the topical indexes are called *digests*. Digests are based on a multi-level outline, beginning with broad topics and moving to narrower subtopics in various areas of law. Cases that have addressed a particular topic or subtopic are listed together at each step of the outline, along with the headnote or headnotes summarizing how the cases addressed the topic. Therefore, when you find a helpful case, you can use the digest to find other cases involving similar issues. Online, the topical indexing systems are also called *headnote systems*.

The West digest system is the most widely used topical index in legal research with print sources; this system is also used on Westlaw. Within the digest system, the *topic* identifies a broad subject area of the law, and the *key number* relates to a subtopic within that area of law. For this reason, the West digest system is also referred to as the Key Number System. Some topics, such as Criminal Law, have over 1,000 key numbers. An example of a topic and key number for cases involving a criminal justice issue is "Searches and Seizures 103.1."[8] The key number 103.1 refers to the subtopic "Warrants—Authority to Issue—In General" under the general topic of "Searches and Seizures." Other West publications, such as secondary sources, will often include topic and key numbers that are relevant to a particular issue.

When West editors create headnotes for a reported case, they assign a topic and key number to each headnote. The headnotes are then listed in the digest under the assigned topic and key numbers. This means that a case will be listed in the digest as many times as it has headnotes. Under individual topic and key numbers, headnotes are arranged by court, with cases from the same court listed in reverse chronological order. A court abbreviation and date at the beginning of each headnote allow you to identify recent or controlling decisions quickly. Note that these abbreviations do not necessarily correspond to abbreviations used for citation purposes.

The main difference between using a print digest and using the headnote or key number system on Westlaw is that print digests, of necessity, are limited in some way—typically by jurisdiction or date, or both. However, because the key number system is uniform, finding cases in one jurisdiction allows you to find similar cases in any jurisdiction using a different digest. On Westlaw, the key number system is not limited in the same way, although researchers will typically limit their searches to a particular jurisdiction. And, of course, the key number system on Westlaw is hyperlinked to the full text of decisions.

Lexis has developed its own topical outline for indexing cases on Lexis Advance; it is not quite as detailed as the West digest system, but serves the same purpose. The headnotes on Lexis Advance are assigned particular topics and subtopics, and can be used to find other cases that were assigned the same topics and subtopics. Bloomberg Law has its own classification system, which is less comprehensive than the indexing systems on Westlaw and Lexis Advance.

---

8. Some key numbers have parentheses and some have decimal points. In general, the parentheses are used for subheadings of an existing key number, while decimals are used to insert new key numbers.

B. Reporters and Digests for Pennsylvania Cases

Pennsylvania State Reports is the official reporter for the Pennsylvania Supreme Court, and is currently published by West.[9] It includes all cases decided by the Pennsylvania Supreme Court.

Cases from the Pennsylvania Supreme Court are also reported in *Atlantic Reporter*, a regional West reporter. *Atlantic Reporter* publishes cases from the courts of the District of Columbia and the following ten states: Connecticut, Delaware, Maine, Maryland, Massachusetts, New Hampshire, New Jersey, Pennsylvania, Rhode Island, and Vermont.[10] For practitioners who do not regularly need to reference cases from other states, West publishes a set of volumes titled *Pennsylvania Reporter*, which are a subset of the pages in the *Atlantic Reporter*. The appearance, pagination, and editorial aids are exactly like those in *Atlantic Reporter*, but the volumes contain only those pages that report cases from Pennsylvania appellate courts. Cases appearing in the *Pennsylvania Reporter* are cited to the *Atlantic Reporter*.

Opinions of the Pennsylvania Superior Court and Pennsylvania Commonwealth Court that are designated as being for publication are published in the *Atlantic Reporter*, which is currently the only reporter in which they appear. Until 1997, opinions of the Superior Court were also published in a reporter called *Pennsylvania Superior Court Reports*. Until 1995, the opinions of the Commonwealth Court were reported in *Pennsylvania Commonwealth Court Reports*. Selected opinions from the Courts of Common Pleas are published in a reporter called *District and County Reports*.

The print digest most commonly used for researching Pennsylvania law is West's *Pennsylvania Digest 2d*. It includes headnotes of cases from state and federal courts in Pennsylvania, as well as United States Supreme Court cases originating in the state or federal courts in Pennsylvania. The *Atlantic Digest 2d* can also be used to locate Pennsylvania state court opinions; however, it does not include federal court decisions.

---

9. *Pennsylvania State Reports* dates back to 1846. West has published *Pennsylvania State Reports* since 1976, beginning with volume 459. Researchers using older volumes will notice a difference in the appearance of the cases before and after that date.

10. West publishes other regional reporters as well: *North Eastern Reporter*, *Pacific Reporter*, *South Eastern Reporter*, *Southern Reporter*, *South Western Reporter*, and *North Western Reporter*. Note that the coverage of each regional reporter is not the same as the composition of the federal circuits, and has no legal significance. The Third Circuit, for instance, does not include most of the states whose decisions are reported in the *Atlantic Reporter*.

In addition to these reporters, some counties publish their own reporters including selected trial court cases. These reporters are not part of the West system. In some cases the only way to obtain a copy of a trial-level opinion will be to request it from the clerk of court.

Reporters publishing opinions of Pennsylvania state courts are listed in Table 2-1.

Table 2-1. Reporters for Pennsylvania Court Cases

Court	Reporter Name	Abbreviation
Pennsylvania Supreme Court	*Pennsylvania State Reports*	Pa.
	Atlantic Reporter	A. A.2d A.3d
Superior Court	*Atlantic Reporter*	See above
	Pennsylvania Superior Court Reports (until 1997)	Pa. Super.
Commonwealth Court	*Atlantic Reporter*	See above
	Pennsylvania Commonwealth Court Reports (until 1995)	Pa. Commw.
Court of Common Pleas	*District and County Reports*	Pa. D. & C. Pa. D. & C.2d Pa. D. & C.3d Pa. D. & C.4th Pa. D. & C.5th

C. Reporters and Digests for Federal Cases

Decisions of the United States Supreme Court are published in three reporters: *United States Reports* (the official reporter); *Supreme Court Reporter* (a West publication); and *United States Supreme Court Reports, Lawyers' Edition* (a LexisNexis publication). The official reporter, *United States Reports*, is the only official source of Supreme Court opinions and should be cited if possible; however, that series frequently publishes cases several years after they are decided. Thus, for recent cases, most lawyers cite the *Supreme Court Reporter*.

Cases decided by the federal circuit courts are published in *Federal Reporter*. Cases that were not designated for publication in *Federal Reporter* might be reprinted in *Federal Appendix*, a relatively new reporter series for "unpublished" cases. Cases appearing in *Federal Appendix* should not be cited as precedent without further research into the rules of your circuit regarding unpublished opinions. The federal circuits do not currently have a uniform approach to unpublished opinions. In the Third Circuit, a majority of the panel of judges deciding a case will determine whether an opinion will be designated as *precedential* or *not precedential*.[11] Opinions designated not precedential have no binding effect; the court does not cite them in other opinions. Litigants can cite them as persuasive or illustrative authority.

Selected cases from the United States District Courts, the federal trial courts, are reported in *Federal Supplement*. Cases arising under federal bankruptcy laws are reported in a separate reporter, *Bankruptcy Reporter*. Selected cases involving the interpretation of federal rules of procedure are reported in *Federal Rules Decisions* and not *Federal Supplement*.

The print digest used most widely for federal law research is West's *Federal Practice Digest*, currently in its fourth series. It includes cases from the Supreme Court, circuit courts, and district courts. West also publishes a digest for United States Supreme Court cases called *United States Supreme Court Digest*. A separate digest for those cases is *United States Supreme Court Digest, Lawyers' Edition*, which corresponds to the similarly titled reporter.

Table 2-2 lists the federal court reporters, along with their citation abbreviations.

III. Finding Judicial Opinions

In many situations you will be able to find relevant judicial opinions by using tools such as statutory annotations. Using the research process set out in Chapter 1 will remind you to consider other alternatives before searching directly for cases. Knowing how to locate opinions directly, however, is still an essential research skill.

Whether you are researching in print sources or online, the process of finding cases involves several steps. The first step is developing a research vocabulary — the list of terms you will use to try to retrieve cases. Developing this research vocabulary should be part of the threshold analysis at the beginning of any research project, but your initial list of terms may need to be ex-

---

11. Internal Operating Procedures of the United States Court of Appeals for the Third Circuit, effective 2017, Rule 5.1–5.7 (available at www2.ca3.uscourts.gov/legacy files/IOPs.pdf).

Table 2-2. Reporters for Federal Court Cases

Court	Reporter Name	Abbreviation
U.S. Supreme Court	*United States Reports*	U.S.
	Supreme Court Reporter	S. Ct.
	United States Supreme Court Reports, Lawyers' Edition	L. Ed. L. Ed. 2d
U.S. Courts of Appeals	*Federal Reporter*	F. F.2d F.3d
U.S. District Courts	*Federal Supplement*	F. Supp. F. Supp. 2d F. Supp. 3d

panded or modified as you search for cases. Be sure to take the time to think of synonyms and related phrases, using a legal dictionary if necessary, so that you do not inadvertently restrict your search more than necessary. As you become more familiar with a particular area of the law, this step will become second nature.

Next, use that vocabulary, either through full-text searching or one of the other methods described next in this chapter, to generate a list of cases. Then, look critically at the results of your search and, if necessary, refine or expand it. The results may be too small if you have omitted synonyms for essential phrases, or may be too extensive if you have searched for especially common terms. Within your search result, identify the cases that are controlling as opposed to those that are merely persuasive.

Finally, update your research. A researcher will only ultimately rely on cases that are still respected authority or "good law." Part IV of this chapter explains updating.

A. Searching for Cases Online

Legal researchers have numerous options for finding cases online, and the options are continually expanding. Most appellate courts now place their opinions online within a relatively short time. In Pennsylvania, the website for the Unified Judicial System provides access to both published and unpublished opinions from the Supreme Court, Superior Court, and Commonwealth Court, often on the day the opinions are released.[12] At the trial court level, some counties publish opinions on their websites; several subscription services also provide access to the opinions published in county reporters. Keep in mind that coverage is not uniform.

Westlaw and Lexis, which have the most extensive coverage and a wide range of editorial enhancements, were for many years the only options for online legal research. In recent years, Bloomberg Law has dramatically increased its coverage and now provides access to both state and federal judicial opinions, as well as court filings. Several lower-cost services, including Casemaker, Fastcase, and VersusLaw, provide good coverage of judicial opinions as well. These lower-cost services have found a market niche by partnering with schools and state bar associations.[13] Google Scholar provides free access to published opinions in state appellate and supreme court cases beginning in 1950; federal court cases beginning in 1923; and U.S. Supreme Court cases beginning in 1791. These services can be a good starting point for finding cases, but none of them provide access to the breadth of research materials available from Westlaw, Lexis Advance, or even Bloomberg Law. In addition, their coverage of unpublished opinions varies.

If you already have a citation, any of these services will allow you to retrieve the opinion by searching for that information in the main search bar. You can also search by party name—you will almost always need some other information to narrow the search, unless the name is unique.

Westlaw also has the option of searching for judicial opinions that actually define a particular term. For example, numerous cases might refer to "recklessness" being an element of a claim, but only a small subset of them will provide a definition of "recklessness" on its own. Judicial definitions can be especially helpful when an important term in a statute is vague. This feature is called Words and Phrases; simply type Words and Phrases in the universal search bar on Westlaw for the link to a search menu, and the search result will be limited to the subset of cases defining the term. You can also construct a field search using "WP" as the field.

1. Full-Text Searching

Full-text searching allows researchers to search directly within the text of judicial opinions, without depending on how those opinions were indexed in

---

12. The website, www.pacourts.us/courts/supreme-court/court-opinions, has basic search filters for retrieving opinions; coverage begins in 1998, but the site is most useful for finding very recent opinions.

13. Casemaker is currently offered to Pennsylvania Bar members as a membership benefit.

a digest. It can be tremendously helpful for finding cases with unique features that might not immediately be apparent from the headnotes assigned to a case. If your research involves general terms, however, your search result may return an unmanageable list. Learning to narrow your search results without missing important authorities is crucial.

One important way to narrow your research is to select the appropriate jurisdiction before you begin, which you can do in any of the online services. In some situations, such as researching a case where there are few cases on point in your jurisdiction, you may need to look elsewhere for persuasive authority. Those situations are the exception rather than the rule, however, particularly when you are beginning a project. In addition, most platforms have numerous filters for narrowing a search result, such as selecting a particular court, adding a date restriction, or searching further for additional terms within the search result.

Two variants of full-text searching exist, each with pros and cons. They were discussed at greater length in the "Research Methods" section of Chapter 1. The first is natural language searching, which is the way most people search for information on the Internet: simply type in a query and the search engine returns a result based on the internal algorithms it uses to recognize key terms. For example, if you were researching a dog owner's liability when the dog bites someone, you could enter "when is an owner liable for injuries caused by a dog" in the search field of the platform you are using. Westlaw, Lexis Advance, and most of the low-cost services allow this type of searching for judicial opinions.

Natural language searching can be a good starting point for finding cases. When your query is general, though, you may retrieve results that contain terms from the query without being directly relevant to the issue you are researching. If your search returns a list of hundreds of cases, look at two or three of the first results to see how your search terms were actually used in those cases and think about rephrasing the query in a way that might narrow the results. Alternatively, if you find even one case that seems to be closely on point, you can use the headnotes in that case to find additional cases rather than continuing to refine the original search result.

The second type of full-text searching is terms and connectors searching, a type of Boolean searching, which uses logic to retrieve documents depending on the relationship between search terms in those documents. This type of searching is available in Westlaw, Lexis Advance, Bloomberg Law, and other providers. Terms and connectors are highly flexible, but it takes practice to construct a search that is focused without being too narrow. Also, the commands or connectors have subtle differences from one platform to another, so take the time to familiarize yourself with the terms and connectors available to you before trying to construct a search.

A terms and connectors search will allow you to include synonyms that might not be included in the result of a natural language search. Using commands or connectors to group your research terms ensures that the result will be focused on the terms you choose. For example, if you were looking for cases involving the "hot pursuit" exception to the warrant requirement, you could search for:

"hot pursuit" and exception and warrant

However, your search result will be much more focused if you search for:

"hot pursuit" /s exception /p warrant

The first search will retrieve documents where the three terms appear anywhere, while the second is much more likely to retrieve cases where the court discussed the warrant requirement in the context of the "hot pursuit" exception. It is worth the time to become adept using terms and connectors, even if you prefer to start your research with a natural language search.

2. Searching by Topic

Searching or browsing by topic rather than performing a full-text search is a good choice when you are researching an unfamiliar area, or when you are having trouble constructing a full-text search.

In Westlaw, you can go to the Key Number System through the "Tools" selection on the main page, and then search for your research terms. Your search will lead you to relevant topic and key numbers, which in turn will lead you to cases. You can also browse individual topics. This is analogous to searching in a print digest, where you move from a general topic to more specific subtopics and then locate cases addressing those subtopics. In addition to using the key number system, you can search in a number of "practice areas" for cases and other authorities in those areas. For example, assume you are interested in the liability of an architect for injuries allegedly caused by the design of a building. Selecting the practice area "Construction" will take you to a screen where you can search for cases, and the result will be restricted to Pennsylvania cases concerning construction law — assuming that you have already set "Pennsylvania" as your default jurisdiction. You can also browse cases from varied jurisdictions within the practice area.

In Lexis Advance, you can choose "Search by topic or headnote" from the "Search" tab on the main search page. This will allow you to select a topic from the index Lexis has developed or to search for a topic using key words. You can browse to a subtopic and then search within that subtopic for reported cases. If you find a helpful case, you can use the Lexis headnotes in that case to locate other cases involving similar issues. Lexis Advance also has "Browse Topics" and "Browse Sources" tabs on the main search page.

Bloomberg Law has a "search and browse" feature allowing you to browse available resources in a number of practice areas.

B. Finding Cases in Print

Using print resources to find cases is not difficult, although it involves additional steps. Simply choose an appropriate digest, search for pertinent topic and key numbers, note the cases indexed under the topic and key numbers you identify, and then retrieve the cases.

The scope of most digests, like the reporters they accompany, is based on jurisdiction. Some digests are geographical or topical. An example of a topical digest is the *Bankruptcy Digest*, which is an index to West's *Bankruptcy Reporter*, a reporter that publishes decisions from the federal bankruptcy courts in all circuits. West also produces a *Decennial Digest* indexing cases from state and federal courts in all jurisdictions for specified time periods. When using any print digest, pay close attention to its coverage. Some digests are cumulative; meaning that they incorporate cases from older series of the same digest; others are not. If a digest is not cumulative, you might need to search in several series to find all relevant cases. Some digests are limited to only state law, or only federal law. Remember that topics and key numbers are consistent throughout all West digests: there is a heading for "Searches and Seizures 103.1" in the *Pennsylvania Digest*, the *Atlantic Digest*, and the *Decennial Digest*, and it refers to the same subtopic in each one.

In print, each West digest includes a Descriptive Word Index. When you do not know which topics and key numbers may be relevant to your research, the Descriptive Word Index allows you to use your research vocabulary to identify relevant topic and key numbers. You can also scan the detailed outline for each broad topic, or Topic Analysis, that appears at the beginning of the topic in the print volumes.

Each print digest in the West system includes a Words and Phrases volume for locating cases that define specific words or phrases. West also produces a multi-volume Words and Phrases set covering all state and federal jurisdictions.

Keep in mind that a search in print resources will normally retrieve only reported, or published, cases, while a search in one of the online platforms will return both reported and unpublished cases. This is not a problem in some research situations, since your goal is normally to find binding authority.

If you cannot locate published cases that are relevant to your situation, however, or if you are trying to predict how a particular court may rule on an issue, then you may want to retrieve unpublished opinions as well.

IV. Verifying that Cases Are Still "Good Law"

An essential step in finding judicial opinions is verifying that you are not basing any conclusions on a case that has been overruled or reversed, or on reasoning that has been called into question by later developments in the law. Researchers use *citators* for this purpose — sources that show all the places one authority has been cited in, or affected by, another authority.

When using Westlaw or Lexis Advance to locate judicial opinions, information from a citator is incorporated into the search result, so you can immediately see whether a case has been called into question. The citator on Westlaw is called KeyCite. It can be used to update cases, as well as statutes and regulations. The citator on Lexis Advance is an online version of Shepard's Citations, which for years was the most widely used and comprehensive citator of legal sources.

KeyCite and Shepard's provide the direct *history* of a decision — whether the decision affirms or reverses an earlier decision, or the decision has itself been affirmed or reversed. In addition, these tools allow you to review a list of all the authorities that have cited a particular decision, and then to filter that list using various criteria. For example, if you are using a case that has been cited hundreds of times because it set out a seminal rule in your jurisdiction, but you are only using it for a narrow point, you can use the headnotes from that case to filter the updating results and find additional cases that raised a particular issue. Reviewing the updating results will tell you more about the *treatment* of the decision — for example, whether it has been followed, distinguished, or criticized by later decisions.

Other platforms have their own updating tools. Bloomberg Law has an updating tool called "BCite"; Casemaker has "CaseCheck+"; and Fastcase has an "Authority Check." Even Google Scholar has an option called "How Cited." If you have retrieved a case using Google Scholar, you can click on the "How Cited" button to retrieve a search result listing other cases that have referred to your case. These citators are useful for flagging situations where you may need to look more closely at a case before relying on it, and can help you find related authorities, but they are not as comprehensive or reliable as KeyCite or Shepard's. In particular, you cannot rely on a negative result — that is, the apparent absence of subsequent history — the way you can rely on a similar result in KeyCite and Shepard's. For this reason, many researchers regard KeyCite and Shepard's as the "gold standard" of updating; even if you use other sources to find cases, you will need to use Westlaw or Lexis Advance for updating. Simply put a citation into the universal search bar on either service; your search result will include whatever treatment and history information is available for that citation.

Do not reflexively rely on the updating tools to tell you how the case has been treated. Even the signals provided in KeyCite and Shepard's are not infallible. For example, you might retrieve a search result where several of the listed cases have "red flags" indicating severely negative treatment. You will not know, until you actually look at the cases, whether the negative treatment affected the court's decision on the particular issue you are researching. Sometimes a case with multiple holdings can be overruled on one point of law, and still remain authoritative on another point. Similarly, you will not know, until you look at the sources of the negative treatment, how much weight to give the negative treatment. Sometimes a case will be marked as having negative treatment because a court in another jurisdiction has rejected it; that may be helpful information to have, but it does not make the case "bad law." Conversely, a case can have no negative treatment at all, but still be outdated. Citators for judicial opinions will only tell you when one opinion has cited or discussed another opinion. The rule of law applied in a particular opinion can be altered or even overruled by later decisions, but unless one of those later decisions cites back to the earlier opinion, the citator will not capture that negative treatment.

Finally, even though online updating tools allow you quickly to check the status of your cases as you are researching, develop the good practice of rechecking your cases before you turn in your work product. In practice, it is not unusual for weeks or months to elapse between the time you first begin research on a particular issue and the time you file something with the court. During that time, anything can happen; a case may have been good law when you found it, but be called into question six months later.

V. Case Analysis

Particularly when full-text searching, a case may initially appear to be similar to the issue you are researching, but closer analysis will reveal that it is not helpful for a number of reasons. Developing strategies for reading and analyzing your search results will help you become a more efficient and effective researcher.

A. The Procedural Posture of a Case and Standards of Review

The *procedural posture* of a case — in other words, the stage of litigation at which an issue was resolved — often affects how helpful it will be in researching a particular issue. In addition, appellate courts are often limited by *standards of review* that require them to defer to certain types of trial court rulings. Think of these as the lenses through which a court will view a legal issue. Some lenses allow the court to look at a larger area; others require the court to focus narrowly.

The following discussion provides a general overview of some procedural stages and standards of review you will encounter when reading cases. For purposes of developing research skills and case reading strategies, what is important is to begin recognizing and noting the different procedural terms and standards.

In civil litigation, a *plaintiff* begins a lawsuit by filing a *complaint* against a *defendant.* The complaint identifies the parties to the lawsuit and the legal claims for relief. The amount of factual detail required in a complaint varies from jurisdiction to jurisdiction. In Pennsylvania state courts, more specific pleading is required than in some other jurisdictions, or in the federal system. However, even in state court cases, the amount of detail available at this stage is much less than will be available at a later stage of litigation.

One possible way a defendant can respond to a complaint is to argue that, even if everything alleged in the complaint is true, the complaint is legally insufficient to entitle the plaintiff to any relief. In Pennsylvania state courts, this response is called a *demurrer.*[14] In federal court, this argument is made in a *motion to dismiss.* In ruling on a demurrer or motion to dismiss, the trial court does not engage in any fact-finding; it simply accepts the complaint as true. A case that was resolved by a demurrer or motion to dismiss, therefore, will be most helpful if the goal of your research is filing a similar motion, or if you are looking for general rules of law.

If the court overrules the demurrer or denies the motion to dismiss, the defendant will have to file an *answer* to the complaint. Then the parties will conduct *discovery,* which is a process allowing each side to gather information about the other's view of the case and the evidence that will be presented at

---

14. A demurrer is one of several possible preliminary objections a defendant can file in response to a complaint under the Pennsylvania Rules of Civil Procedure. *See* Pa. R. Civ. P. 1028.

trial. Sometimes the discovery process will lead to the filing of pretrial motions. For example, the parties might identify their expert witnesses in the discovery process. The defendant might then file a motion seeking to exclude the testimony of one of the plaintiff's expert witnesses. The court will typically rule on the motion after a hearing.

After the discovery process, either party may file a motion for *summary judgment* asking the court to decide in that party's favor without holding a trial. The standard for ruling on a motion for summary judgment is different from the standard for ruling on a demurrer or motion to dismiss; instead of accepting the allegations of the complaint as true, the court will consider the evidence that has been developed during the discovery process and will decide whether that evidence creates enough of a dispute to require a trial. Therefore, opinions issued after a motion for summary judgment often provide information about the factual context of the court's decision.

When the trial judge grants a motion that ends a case, the losing party can appeal. The appealing party is called the *appellant*; the other party is the *appellee*. In deciding an appeal from an order granting a motion, the appellate court is deciding whether the trial judge was correct in issuing the order at that stage of the litigation. If the appellate court agrees with the decision of the trial judge, it will *affirm*. If not, the court will *reverse* the order granting the motion and in some instances *remand* the case back to the trial court.

Once a trial has been held, it is fairly rare—although not impossible—for the resulting decision to be overturned on appeal. This is, in part, because our judicial system gives great deference to the role of a jury as the finder of fact. Even when a case is heard in a *bench trial,* meaning that the judge serves as the fact-finder and no jury is present, the judge's findings of fact will receive great deference from the appellate court and are not easy to overturn. For this reason, many reported appellate cases are appeals of orders granting various motions, and appeals after a trial typically focus on errors of law.

On appeal, the applicable standard of review[15] will often control the outcome. For example, assume that the trial court makes a ruling that is considered to be something within its discretion, such as a ruling admitting certain evidence. On appeal, in addition to considering whatever substantive rule of law the trial court applied, the appellate court will also consider the principle that these types of rulings are only reversed if the trial court *abused its discretion.*

---

15. A comprehensive description of standards of review is beyond the scope of this text, but numerous sources exist for understanding them, including judicial opinions themselves.

The appellate court will not substitute its own judgment for the judgment of the trial court, but instead will ask whether the trial court's conclusion was unreasonable or the result of a misapplication of the law. If the conclusion is not manifestly unreasonable, it will be allowed to stand. In contrast, if a complaint is legally insufficient, the trial court does not have the discretion to let the lawsuit proceed. On appeal, the appellate court will not ask whether the trial court abused its discretion, but instead whether the court made an *error of law*. The appellate court will answer that question by applying the same test the trial court used and reaching its own conclusion without deferring to the trial court.

This discussion has focused on civil procedure, but the underlying principle applies to research in criminal law as well: the stage of the case at which an issue arises will often affect how it is analyzed and, therefore, how helpful it will be in your research. The legal standard a trial court will apply when ruling on a motion to suppress evidence before trial is different from the standard the court will apply if the defendant requests a new trial after an adverse jury verdict. An appellate court, in turn, will use a different standard of review depending on the type of ruling being appealed.

B. Assessing the Relevance and Weight of Opinions

Ideally, if you have constructed your search carefully, your research will not produce results that are not legally relevant—that is, results that do not apply a principle of law related to your research issue. When full-text searching, there is always a risk of retrieving cases that mention, but do not discuss, a particular legal issue. If you skim the first several cases in your search result and more than one or two of them do not actually discuss the principle(s) you are researching, stop and refine your search.

Cases that are factually relevant can be more difficult to identify without reading the case closely. The most helpful cases will present legally significant facts—facts affecting the court's decision on the issues—that are similar or analogous to the facts of your client's situation. You can use the reasoning of those cases to predict how the court will apply the law to your client. If a relevant case reaches a conclusion favorable to your client, your goal will be to emphasize the similarities between the facts of the case and your client's situation. If the case reaches an adverse conclusion, you will try to distinguish the facts or the reasoning of the case to justify a different result in your client's situation.

What facts are legally significant depends on the case. Whether a driver was texting shortly before an automobile accident may be critical in a lawsuit brought by a crash victim, but is not likely to be legally significant if the driver is prosecuted for driving under the influence because a blood test at the hospital after the accident revealed a blood alcohol level over the legal limit.

Once you determine that a case is relevant to some portion of your analysis, you must decide how heavily it will weigh in your analysis. The first consideration is the court that decided the case. Authority from the highest court in a jurisdiction will always be binding on lower courts in that jurisdiction. The Pennsylvania Superior Court and Pennsylvania Commonwealth Court must follow the decisions of the Pennsylvania Supreme Court; the trial courts, in turn, must follow decisions of the Superior Court and Commonwealth Court. Whether authority from the intermediate appellate court in another jurisdiction is binding or merely persuasive will depend on the rules of the jurisdiction where you are researching.

In addition, courts apply the principle of *stare decisis*, which means "to stand by things decided,"[16] to ensure consistency. This means that courts normally follow their own prior opinions, unless a good reason exists for deviating from the prior opinions. This requirement is limited to the courts within one jurisdiction. The Pennsylvania Superior Court should follow its own earlier decisions in deciding new cases, but does not have to follow decisions from other states. If a court decides not to continue following its own earlier cases, it is usually because of some social or economic change that undermines the reasoning of the earlier cases, or because a statute has been enacted that supersedes the earlier cases. Sometimes, rather than departing from a line of earlier cases, a court will find a factual distinction that supports a different result in a new situation without disregarding the principle of *stare decisis*.

Another consideration is whether the legal principles set out in the opinion are actually the court's holding, meaning the court's resolution of a matter at issue in the case. Statements or observations included in the opinion, but not necessary to resolve a matter at issue, are referred to as *dicta* and are not binding. For example, a court in a custody dispute may hold that Mr. and Mrs. Doe are not entitled to visitation with their former foster child. In reaching that decision, the court may observe that if a few facts had been different, it would have granted visitation to Mr. and Mrs. Doe. That observation is not binding on future courts, though it may be cited as persuasive authority.

A final consideration is whether the opinion was supported by the entire panel or court that decided the case. The opinion supported by a majority of

---

16. *Black's Law Dictionary* 1626 (Bryan A. Garner ed., 10th ed., Thomson West 2014).

the judges is called the *majority opinion*. The majority opinion is the only opinion with precedential value. An opinion written to agree with the outcome of the majority, but not the reasoning, is called a *concurring opinion*. When a majority of judges or justices agree on the outcome, but not the reasoning, the result is a *plurality opinion*. Because a plurality opinion does not result in a clear majority, it may have limited precedential value.

Concurring opinions can have persuasive value, but do not represent the judgment of the court. Opinions written by judges or justices who disagree with the outcome, or *dissenting opinions*, can have persuasive value as well. Complicated combinations of concurrences and dissents are seen more often in U.S. Supreme Court decisions than in state court decisions.

C. Preparing to Present Your Analysis

Effective legal research often involves both synthesis and reduction: synthesis of the controlling rule from a number of sources, and then reduction of that rule into its components to ensure you have fully analyzed how the rule applies to your research situation. Sometimes the controlling rule will be stated in a single place, such as a single, binding judicial opinion, or a single statute, and all you will have to do is determine how different cases illustrate various components of the rule. Sometimes, however, you will have to piece together the holdings of several cases, or combine a statutory provision with the holdings of several cases, to be able to state the legal rule you are applying.

Even when the controlling rule is stated clearly in one case, it is unlikely you will find one case that addresses all aspects of the rule. Many rules have several elements or factors. *Elements* are required subparts of the rule; *factors* are considerations that are potentially important, but not required. In addition, some rules are *balancing tests* that require some factors to be weighed against others. For example, to prevail on a claim of negligence, a plaintiff has to prove four elements: that the defendant had a duty, the defendant breached that duty, the breach caused harm to the plaintiff, and the plaintiff suffered damages as a direct result. If any one of those elements is missing, the claim will fail. When a court is deciding whether a duty was present, however, the court will analyze several factors. Even if one factor is not present, the weight of the others may be sufficient to find that a duty exists.

When a test with required elements is at issue, and the court decides that one required element is missing, it often will not discuss the other elements in its opinion. Similarly, an opinion may be limited to discussing one or two factors that the court found determinative based on the facts of the case, and will not discuss other potential factors that had no effect on the outcome.

Because effective legal research requires synthesis, the work product generated from your research must be more than a case-by-case summary of your results. The memo or brief you eventually write will be organized according to the synthesized rule of law you are applying. Because effective application of legal rules to a client's situation requires reduction, you must be able to distinguish the components of a synthesized rule. Therefore, from the beginning stages of your research, you should be thinking about the components of the rule you are applying and using those components as an outline to organize your notes and sources. If a case is helpful in illustrating more than one component of the rule, it will be listed at more than one place in your notes.

Throughout your research, be aware that you have an ethical duty to ensure that the court knows about a case directly on point, even if the outcome of that case is adverse to your client. As a practical matter, this means you should also acknowledge adverse authority in a memorandum, even if the memorandum will not be filed with a court. Therefore, if you find a case that is both legally and factually relevant, you should include it in your notes and outline regardless of the outcome.

D. Reading and Analyzing Cases

The following suggestions for reading cases are just that—suggestions. With experience, you will find which strategies for reading and analyzing cases work best for you.

- Search engines often present results in relevance order by default, meaning the results that contained the highest occurrence of your search terms will appear first. This can be useful for assessing your search and making refinements. When you are ready to read more than a few cases, however, it is often a good idea to read them in reverse chronological order. This approach will avoid the problem of spending time taking notes on an older case, only to realize it has become outdated in light of later legal developments.
- Start with binding authority. If your search retrieved unpublished opinions or cases from outside your jurisdiction, skip them or set them aside to return to them later, if necessary.
- Use the synopsis and headnotes to determine quickly whether a case seems to be on point. Remember that one case may discuss several issues of law, only one or two of which may interest you.

- The synopsis and headnotes will often indicate the procedural posture of the case and the standard of review the court applied. If your research involves a particular type of motion or ruling, set aside cases that were decided on a different basis; you can return to them at a later stage to look for any persuasive reasoning they might contain.
- If a case appears to be relevant, skim the entire case quickly. Then re-read it, focusing on the portion or portions that are relevant to your research.
- Take notes on each relevant case. Write down the holding of the case, the legally significant facts, and the reasoning. Even if you do not follow the formal structure of a "case brief," taking notes will help ensure that you are reading the case carefully and understanding key portions. Merely highlighting a printed page is not a substitute for note-taking. Cases can be downloaded in PDF form and annotated without printing them out. Experiment to see whether reviewing printed copies is more effective for you.
- As you take notes, identify how each case fits into the rule of law you are applying or analyzing. For example, if you are researching whether your client had a duty of care, identify the factor or factors each case emphasized and whether a duty was found. Taking specific notes as you read will help you identify any factors or elements in your rule that are not addressed in the cases you have located, and will help you avoid gaps in your analysis.
- Try to formulate a concise statement of the principle(s) for which you might cite each case as you read it. This does not mean you will actually cite each case in your written work, but it is a useful way to make sure you understand the holding.
- Keep a law dictionary handy to check unfamiliar terms.

Chapter 3

Statutes

State legislatures and Congress pass thousands of statutes each year addressing a wide array of subjects. Many situations requiring a lawyer's advice involve statutory interpretation instead of common law principles. Even common law questions often have statutory angles, such as a statute of limitations issue. You should determine early in your research whether your project will require consulting statutes.

This chapter includes a basic overview of codified statutes, followed by an explanation of how to use Pennsylvania's annotated and unannotated codes. The discussion of statutes is followed by an introduction to local ordinances and how to find them. A brief explanation of federal statutory research also is included. The chapter concludes with an overview of statutory construction and the relationship between statutes and other types of authority.

I. Overview

The essential tools of statutory research are similar from one jurisdiction to another, although specific publications vary. When a legislature first passes a law, it is typically published as a *slip law*. Slip laws are published chronologically as they are enacted and, in many jurisdictions, are the definitive source for the law currently in force. At the end of each legislative session, the slip laws for that session are compiled in chronological order and published in bound volumes, which are generically referred to as *session laws*. The publication titles of session laws vary by jurisdiction. Although slip laws and session laws play a role in statutory research, they are difficult to use because they are arranged by date rather than by topic.

Codified statutes solve that problem by arranging statutes according to the topics they cover, making it easier to find relevant laws. Codified statutes typically include at least cursory information on the history of each statutory section that allows a researcher to trace the development of the statute, but codified statutes can also be *annotated* with more extensive legislative history information, research references, and notes of decisions that have interpreted or applied various statutory sections. Although *unannotated* statutes, which only include the statutory text and basic legislative history, have a role in research, most statutory research is done with annotated statutes.

In most jurisdictions, researchers have access to both official and unofficial, or privately published, statutes. An *official* codification of statutes is one that is compiled and published under the authority of jurisdictional government rather than by a private publisher. Official codifications are typically not annotated.

II. Pennsylvania Statutory Research

When the Pennsylvania General Assembly enacts laws, the bills are first published individually as *slip laws*. At the end of the legislative session, all the slip laws from that session are bound into one or more volumes titled the *Laws of Pennsylvania*, which are unofficially referred to as the *pamphlet laws*. Most pamphlet laws are then codified. Examples of laws that would not be codified include enacted budget and appropriations bills, because those laws are not of a general and permanent nature.

Statutory research in Pennsylvania has some unique features because Pennsylvania did not begin to publish official codified statutes until after most other states had already done so. For many years, researchers relied on a private publication, *Purdon's Pennsylvania Statutes Annotated*, for codified statutes. The Commonwealth began publishing official codified statutes in the 1970s. The official, unannotated version of the codified statutes is titled *Pennsylvania Consolidated Statutes*. The official statutes are incomplete, however, because not all statutory law has been consolidated into the official version. In addition, when Pennsylvania began to publish the official codification of the statutes, the official version did not use the same taxonomy as *Purdon's*. There was some overlap, but some titles were numbered and arranged differently. For these reasons, *Pennsylvania Consolidated Statutes* must be consulted together with *Pennsylvania Statutes Annotated*. This sounds more complicated than it is in practice because, both in print and online, the two versions can be searched together. Whether you are using the annotated or unannotated statutes, you must pay attention to whether you are retrieving a section that has been recodified in *Pennsylvania Consolidated Statutes* or, instead, a section in *Pennsylvania Statutes Annotated*, and cite the section accordingly. The most important thing to remember is the codes work in a complementary, not competitive, manner.

A. Annotated Codes

In Pennsylvania statutory research, the most often used resource is an unofficial, annotated publication titled *Purdon's Pennsylvania Statutes Annotated and Consolidated Statutes Annotated*, which is published by West in print and available on Westlaw. This set is often referred to simply as *Purdon's*.[1] In addition to statutes, the series includes the Pennsylvania Constitution and court rules. *Purdon's* also includes "disposition tables," which tell you where to find statutes that have been recodified in *Pennsylvania Consolidated Statutes*. Lexis has its own version of the annotated codes.

In the annotated codes, the statutory text of each section is followed by annotations and other editorial notes that aid in research. These annotations include historical notes, which show the derivation of the current statute and explain some of its development. The date the statute was enacted and the dates of subsequent amendments are noted along with the session law citations. The historical notes provide a springboard to legislative history research, which is discussed in the next chapter.

The annotations also include cross-references to other statutes and regulations that relate to the statute you are researching. References to topical outlines used for finding related case law and secondary sources discussing the statute may be included as well, depending on the publisher.

Finally, state cases, federal cases, and attorney general opinions that have interpreted or applied the statute are listed in Notes of Decisions (West) or Case Notes (Lexis). These notes are arranged alphabetically by topic. You can skim these summary notes to get a preliminary idea of which cases would be most helpful in analyzing your statutory issue.

1. Annotated Codes in Print

Unless you are starting with a statutory citation, the easiest way to begin using *Purdon's* in print is to search the paperback index volumes for terms related to your issue. When you have identified relevant statutory sections in the index, locate them in the hardbound volumes using the title and section number.

---

1. Although *Purdon's* is a West publication, it is the generic term used when referencing an annotated, codified version of Pennsylvania's statutes. If instructed to find something in *Purdon's* but you use Lexis Advance, simply use the annotated statutes available on Lexis Advance.

Another entry point to the code is the table of contents. Each title has a table of contents. If you are sure which title you need to search, you can go directly to that title within the hardbound volumes.

Purdon's in print is updated with paper pocket parts and semi-annual pamphlets. Depending on how recently a bound volume was last reprinted, it is not unusual for the current version of a statutory provision to be in the pocket part rather than in the bound volume. For this reason, you should always check the pocket part or pamphlet supplements to ensure you are using the current version of the statute.

Purdon's also contains a number of tables, including statutory cross-reference tables that allow you to find citations to statutory provisions if all you have is a pamphlet law number. The Popular Name Table will allow you to find the citation to a statute if all you know is its name, such as the Historic Preservation Act.

2. Annotated Codes Online

The content of the online versions of *Pennsylvania Statutes Annotated and Consolidated Statutes Annotated* mirrors that of the print version. The online versions are updated much more frequently than the print versions and incorporate amendments into the statutory text, so you do not have to rely on pocket parts and pamphlets. Although they are typically current to at least the end of the former calendar year, remember that further updating may be necessary during the legislative session to make sure no very recent changes have occurred. Tracking current legislation is discussed below.

To locate the annotated versions of the codes in Westlaw, look in the general content category *Statutes & Court Rules;* then filter to Pennsylvania. Westlaw will take you directly into the general table of contents of the *Purdon's* set. Once there, you can select a relevant title, full-text search both codes together, full-text search specific titles and chapters in each code to narrow your focus, or use the *Index* or *Popular Name Table* in the Tools & Resources box on the right.

To locate the annotated versions of the codes using Lexis Advance, look in the general content category *Statutes and Legislation;* then filter to Pennsylvania. Under the heading *Codes,* you can either select the title *Pennsylvania Statutes Annotated,* which will take you directly to a full-text search screen, or open the table of contents icon to browse *Pennsylvania Statutes Annotated* and *Consolidated Statutes Annotated.* Once in the table of contents, you can full-text search both codes together or separately. Although Lexis has started adding indices and popular name tables for some content, neither are available for *Pennsylvania Statutes Annotated* or *Consolidated Statutes Annotated* as of the revision date of this book.

You can also search for statutory provisions directly from the universal search bar on both Westlaw and Lexis Advance, using either a natural language search or a terms and connectors search.[2] For example, if you were researching the statute of limitations for a defamation claim under Pennsylvania law, you could select Pennsylvania as your jurisdiction and enter "statute of limitations for defamation" in the universal search bar. The search result will include both cases and statutes, along with numerous other sources.

Regardless of how you find a particular statutory provision in Westlaw or Lexis Advance, your search result will also include information from the citators on each platform (KeyCite on Westlaw, or Shepard's on Lexis Advance) on how the provision has been treated by subsequent legislation, as well as how it has been cited.

Citators will signal you when a statute has negative treatment of which you should be aware—for example, if a statute has been held unconstitutional, preempted, repealed, superseded, or recently amended. Their importance cannot be overstated, so be sure to pay attention to the citator symbols assigned to statutes. On Westlaw, look for a red or yellow flag. Clicking on this flag will take you to the sources that treat the statute negatively. If there is no negative treatment, you can use the other KeyCite links—Notes of Decisions, History, Citing References, or Context and Analysis—to find out how that statute has been cited and applied. On Lexis Advance, look for a red exclamation point in the Shepard's box to the right of the statute, which will take you to the sources containing negative treatment of the statute. Lexis Advance also has links for Legislative History, Citing Decisions, and Other Citing Sources. Both services have tools for filtering a KeyCite or Shepard's report—for example, if a statutory provision has been cited by hundreds of cases, you can narrow the result by date or jurisdiction.

B. Unannotated Codes

The official version of the code contains only the statutory text and, in some cases, limited notes about enactment of each statute. Because *Pennsylvania Consolidated Statutes* does not contain annotations, it is not typically used for researching the statutes. Typically, you use *Pennsylvania Consolidated Statutes* when you already have a statutory citation and simply need to verify the official language.

---

2. These searches were compared in Section IV of Chapter 1, The Legal Research Process.

Pennsylvania Consolidated Statutes is published in print in looseleaf form by the Legislative Reference Bureau and updated annually with changes in the current laws. Statutes may be amended during a legislative session, but those amendments will not be reflected in print until the following annual update. You must use session laws to ensure you are using the most current version of the statute. Each title in the print version of the official code has an index. If the relevant title is known or can be ascertained, the title index can be used to find relevant statutory provisions.

Online, *Pennsylvania Consolidated Statutes* is accessible for free on the General Assembly's website.[3] You can full-text search the code using keywords. Advanced operators (terms and connectors searching) can be used for more targeted searching. You can search using title, chapter, and section numbers. You also can browse hyperlinked metadata or PDF versions of each title's table of contents.

Westlaw publishes an open access, unannotated version of unconsolidated *Purdon's Pennsylvania Statutes* on its government portal.[4] As with the official statutes, this version is typically used when you are verifying statutory language rather than doing broader research.

In addition to these sources, Bloomberg Law and Casemaker provide access to searchable, but unannotated, versions of Pennsylvania statutes.

C. Recently Enacted Legislation

Although statutory research typically relies on annotated codes rather than session laws, the chronological laws still fill several essential roles. You will need to work with session laws when you are researching a law that did not become part of the official code, such as an appropriations bill or budget. If annotated versions of statutes are not readily available, you may need to consult session laws in connection with the official statutes to determine the effective date of a particular statutory revision. Session laws are also useful for updating statutes during or immediately after a legislative session, before any changes have appeared in the codified versions of the statutes. Finally, because different sections of a law can be codified in different locations in the official statutes,

---

3. The General Assembly home page is www.legis.state.pa.us. The site also has links to an online version of *Laws of Pennsylvania* and the *Pennsylvania Code*, which is a set of administrative rules.

4. The main page of Westlaw's government portal is govt.westlaw.com; from there, you can access the *Unofficial Purdon's Pennsylvania Statutes* and browse the table of contents, search for a citation, or search for a phrase.

it is sometimes helpful to read the full text of an act rather than piecing together sections that have been codified separately.

1. Laws of Pennsylvania

Pennsylvania laws are first published individually as slip laws upon enact-ment. Slip laws include the text of the statute, the title, the effective date, and other information, and they show how any existing statute was modified by bracketing text that was removed and underscoring new language. The number assigned to an act after it becomes law reflects its chronological position, so Act No. 1 from 2017 means it was the first act to become law in 2017.

At the end of each legislative session, the slip laws are compiled chronolog-ically and published in bound volumes titled *Laws of Pennsylvania*; hence, the term session laws. In practice, the term "session law" often generically refers to both slip laws and session laws. When the session laws are published in *Laws of Pennsylvania*, they are assigned a pamphlet law number, which indicates where they appear in *Laws of Pennsylvania*. This explains why Pennsylvania session laws are sometimes referred to as the pamphlet laws. In addition to the printed volumes, *Laws of Pennsylvania* are available on Westlaw, Lexis Ad-vance, and the General Assembly website.

2. Finding Recent Changes to Existing Laws

To research recently enacted laws or to find recent changes to existing laws in print, refer to *Purdon's Pennsylvania Legislative Service*, which is published by West. During legislative sessions, this service is published as a series of pa-perback volumes, allowing for quick publication.

To locate session laws in Westlaw, look in the general content category *Pro-posed & Enacted Legislation*; then filter to Pennsylvania. Depending on how recently the legislation was enacted, select either *Enacted Legislation (Session Laws)*, which usually contains laws from the current legislative session, or *Historical Sessions Laws* in the Tools & Resources box on the right for older session laws.

To locate session laws using Lexis Advance, look in the general content cat-egory *Statutes and Legislation*; then filter to Pennsylvania. Under the heading *Public Laws/ALS*, select *Pennsylvania Advanced Legislative Service*.

The General Assembly's website provides open access to recently enacted legislation. Look for the Legislation tab on the website. Then select *by Legislation Enacted*. You can search for general legislation, appropriation acts, vetoed bills, joint resolutions, and other documents by year or act number. The Legislative

Reference Bureau is working on an ongoing project to digitize and add recent and historical session laws to their website as well. Although the collection of *Laws of Pennsylvania* available on their website is incomplete, it is another source for pamphlet laws.

D. Pending Legislation

In practice, research will often be an ongoing process spanning weeks, months, or longer. When this is the case, it is crucial to be aware of pending legislation that, if enacted, may change the statutory language upon which you are relying.

Fortunately, online research services, both paid and open access, provide tools to help you track pending legislation. Because the online options for tracking pending legislation are superior to print services, this section will not cover print services.

The citators on Westlaw and Lexis Advance can be used to alert you to pending legislation that might affect the statutory provision you are viewing. They also provide alert services you can customize to email you if any pending legislation related to that statute is enacted.

For Pennsylvania statutes, Westlaw is more effective at alerting you of pending legislation when viewing a statute. Look for a yellow flag next to the title of the statute you are researching. Clicking on this yellow flag will take you to all pending legislation that may impact that statute. To set up an alert, look for the bell icon in the upper right of the tool ribbon just above the statute. Clicking on this bell will take you to a form to create a custom alert that can be set to email you of any changes in the statute on a weekly, biweekly, or monthly basis.

Unfortunately, as of the date of this edition, Lexis Advance has not activated the Shepard's function for alerting you of pending legislation when viewing a statute. You can create a custom alert, however, to receive a notification when newly enacted legislation has changed a particular statute. The process for setting up an alert on Lexis Advance is very similar to the process on Westlaw. Look for a bell icon on the top left of your screen next to the citation of the statute you are viewing. Clicking this bell will take you to a form similar to Westlaw's alert form with one noticeable difference: you can set the alert to run and notify you *daily*, weekly, or monthly.

The Pennsylvania General Assembly website provides several options for tracking pending legislation. Look for a link to sign up for the *PaLegis Notifications* service. You can opt to receive daily session updates on all legislative action the previous day, activity updates for specific committees, or updates for specific bills. You can also sign up to receive instant updates on session information via numerous RSS feeds.[5]

III. Local Ordinances

Local government entities in Pennsylvania are municipalities, which in turn can be cities, boroughs, townships, or school districts. The area of municipal law, or the relationship between the state and its municipalities, is a specialty in itself. Within certain limits, municipalities can pass ordinances, or laws of local application. Ordinances are only binding within a particular municipality.

Typical examples of areas that are usually governed by local ordinances are animal control and zoning. So, for example, one township might have a "leash law" prohibiting dog owners from allowing their dogs to run loose, while a neighboring township might not have a similar ordinance. Issues such as curfews and property maintenance are also frequently the subject of local ordinances. Less frequently, a municipality might choose to augment state law in a particular area, such as by enacting an anti-discrimination ordinance or an environmental ordinance that is stricter than what statewide laws provide.

Local ordinances are collected together and published as "codes." The best way to find the text of local ordinances is online. City and county websites frequently provide access to the ordinances in effect there. In addition, a number of websites provide access to selected codes, including eCode360, Municode, and American Legal Publishing. Westlaw, Lexis Advance, and Bloomberg Law also provide access to municipal codes. In some cases, you may need to contact the municipality directly to obtain a current version of a specific ordinance.

At the local level, decisions applying the text of local ordinances are not widely reported. However, if the decisions are appealed to the Court of Common Pleas or, from there, to the Commonwealth Court, the resulting decisions may be reported, or may be available as unpublished decisions. If your research involves a challenge to a local law, however — perhaps on the grounds that the municipality exceeded its authority in enacting it — then you are researching an issue of municipal law. Numerous secondary sources are available in this area of the law, and it is one of the broad topic areas on both Westlaw and Lexis Advance. Basic information on municipal law in Pennsylvania is available

---

5. The General Assembly also posts legislative updates via its twitter feed — @PaLegis.

on a number of websites, including the Local Government Commission of the Pennsylvania Assembly, the Pennsylvania Department of Community and Economic Development, and the Pennsylvania Municipal League.

IV. Federal Statutory Research

Federal statutory research is similar to state statutory research. When Congress enacts laws, those laws are first published individually as slip laws (either *public laws* or *private laws*). At the end of the legislative session, all the slip laws from that session are bound chronologically into volumes and published as the *United States Statutes at Large*; hence, these are the session laws. Session laws of a general and permanent nature are then codified.

The official version of the codified statutes is titled *United States Code* (USC). The USC is an *unannotated* code; it includes the statutory text and basic information about the legislative history of each section. West and Lexis each publish unofficial, annotated federal codes.

A. Annotated Codes

Annotated, unofficial codes are used most often to research federal statutes, both because the annotated codes contain more research information and because the publication schedule for USC is quite slow. The two annotated codes for federal statutes are the *United States Code Annotated* (USCA), published by West, and the *United States Code Service* (USCS), published by Lexis.

The annotated codes include the statutory text of each section, historical notes about the legislative history of each statute, cross-references to other relevant statutes and regulations, cases that have applied or interpreted statutory provisions, and secondary sources discussing the statute may be included as well. Although structured similarly, the USCA and USCS are not identical because the publishers reference their own proprietary publications. Some practitioners prefer one publication over the other but, for purposes of finding statutory text and references to other sources, both are helpful.

As is the case with *Purdon's*, if you do not have a citation, the best entry points for using the USCA and the USCS in print are the table of contents, indices, and popular name tables. The USCA and the USCS are updated using pocket parts and supplementary pamphlets, so make it a habit check those for recent changes.

To locate the USCA in Westlaw, look in the general content category *Statutes & Court Rules;* then select *United States Code Annotated (USCA)* under the heading *Federal.* To find relevant statutes, use the same research techniques outlined in the section discussing using annotated codes online for Pennsylvania.

To locate the USCS in Lexis Advance, look in the general content category *Statutes and Legislation;* then filter to *Federal.* Under the heading *Codes,* you can select the title *USCS—United States Code Service,* which will take you directly to a full-text search screen, open the table of contents icon to browse each title on a more granular level or full-text search, or select the *USCS Popular Names Table.* Although Lexis Advance has started adding indices for some content, the index for the USCS was not available as of the revision date of this book.

B. Unannotated Code

The Office of the Law Revisions Counsel of the United States of the House of Representatives (OLRC) prepares the *United States Code,* which is the unannotated codification of federal laws of a general and permanent nature.

The USC contains the text and basic legislative history of each statute. As with *Pennsylvania Consolidated Statutes,* researchers typically use the USC either when they already have a statutory citation and simply need to verify the statutory text or do not have access to an annotated version of the code. Although not as useful for research as an annotated version of the code, citation conventions require the USC to be cited whenever possible. Because the publication schedule is slow, it is sometimes necessary to cite to one of the annotated codes when citing relatively recent enactments.

The print version of the USC is formally republished in its entirety every six years by the U.S. Government Publishing Office (GPO) after it has been prepared by the OLRC. Although the print version of the USC is updated with annual, cumulative supplements between editions, it is important to remember there often is a lag time between when a law is enacted and its publication in print. This is why slip laws and session laws are important for researching statutes in print.

The USC also is available online. The GPO website for government documents provides open access to the USC.[6] You can use the Browse by Category feature to locate the USC under the *Bills and Statutes* heading, or you can use the *Advanced* search tab to full-text search using keywords. The OLRC's website also provides open access to the USC. You can search using the title and section number, browse the table of contents, or full-text search using keywords.[7]

---

6. The GPO site, Govinfo.gov, has links to a wide variety of federal information.
7. The OLRC version is available at uscode.house.gov/.

Finally, Bloomberg Law and some of the low-cost services also provide access to unannotated federal statutes.

C. Recently Enacted Legislation

In the federal system, most slip laws are assigned a *public law* number upon enactment. A public law number indicates the number of the Congress that passed the law and the chronological order of the law when passed. For example, public law 107-313 was the 313th law passed by the 107th Congress, but it was passed in November 2002. Like pamphlet laws in Pennsylvania, federal public laws are the text of a statute as it was enacted, but not necessarily as it will be codified in *United States Code*. Federal session laws are officially compiled and published in *United States Statutes at Large* at the end of each Congressional session.

Because public laws are not immediately codified, you may need to reference the federal slip laws or session laws to ensure you are using the most current version of a statute.[8]

D. Pending Legislation

You will often need to check for pending legislation that, if enacted, would change the statutory language upon which you are relying. For federal laws, online research services, paid and open access, provide comprehensive *citator* services to help you track pending legislation and create alerts if pending legislation is enacted. Citators also signal other negative treatment of which you should be aware, so be sure to pay attention to the citator symbols assigned to statutes. Again, print will not be covered in this section because the online tools are superior to print services.

On Westlaw, the citator symbols for federal statutes function the same as they do for Pennsylvania statutes. Look for the yellow flag, which indicates proposed legislation, and create an alert for your statute using the bell icon.

For federal statutes on Lexis Advance, the citator symbols that indicate pending legislation are active. Look for a yellow exclamation point in the Shepard's box to the right of the statute, which will take you to the relevant pending legislation. You can create an alert for tracking changes to a federal statute using the previously discussed bell icon.

---

8. Public laws are available on the Congress.gov website; public laws and the *Statutes at Large* are available on Govinfo.gov.

Westlaw and Lexis use the same symbols previously discussed to indicate negative treatment of a statute. Again, look for a red flag (Westlaw) or a red exclamation point (Lexis Advance) to view the sources containing negative treatment of the statute.

Congress.gov, the official website for federal legislative information, is administered by the Library of Congress and provides open access to pending legislation and alert notifications. Look for the *Sign In* link at the top right of the website, register for a free account, and sign in. You can search for pending legislation using either a known bill number or subject-related keywords. Once you locate pending legislation you want to track, look for the *Get alerts* link directly beneath the title of the proposed legislation. Clicking on this link will create an alert. You will be updated about activity related to that legislation as it moves through the legislative process.

V. Statutory Interpretation

Statutory interpretation begins with a careful reading of the statute. Because statutory concepts often are complex and written in long sentences, a careful reading of a statute may require time and patience. Be sure to read the statute yourself; you should never rely on an article's summary of a statute or even a court's quote of a statute as a replacement for reading the statute.

Even if a narrow provision seems to answer your research question, skim through the entire statute to put that provision in context. Review sections containing definitions and effective dates. Note any important requirements or exceptions, as well as provisions that clearly do not apply to your client's circumstances. Pay special attention to words that affect the scope of the statute, like "and" — "or"; "all" — "some"; "must" — "may." Then read the statute again, focusing this time on the relevant portions. If the statute is complex, outlining the rule presented in the statute may increase your understanding of it. Consider the example of the Medical Good Samaritan Civil Immunity law, 42 Pa. Cons. Stat. Ann. §8331(a):

> Any physician or any other practitioner of the healing arts or any registered nurse, licensed by the state, who happens by chance upon the scene of an emergency or who arrives on the scene of an emergency by reason of serving on an emergency call panel or similar committee of a county medical society or who is called to the scene of an emergency by the police or other duly constituted officers of a government

unit or who is present when an emergency occurs and who, in good faith, renders emergency care at the scene of the emergency, shall not be liable for any civil damages as a result of any acts or omissions by such physician or practitioner or registered nurse in rendering the emergency care, except any acts or omissions intentionally designed to harm or any grossly negligent acts or omissions which result in harm to the person receiving emergency care.

What must be true for a person to be immune from liability under this statute?

- the person must act in good faith, and
- the emergency care must be given because
  - the person arrived upon the scene of the emergency by chance, or
  - the person was serving on an emergency call panel or similar committee, or
  - the person was called to the scene of the emergency by the police or other government officers, or
  - the person was present when the emergency occurred, and
- the person must render emergency care at the scene of the emergency, and
- the person must not perform any acts or omissions intentionally designed to harm the victim, and
- the person must not perform any grossly negligent acts or omissions which result in harm to the victim

Review the statute frequently as you continue your research. This review will ensure that you remember the exact language of the statute and will allow you to bring to subsequent readings greater insight based on your increased knowledge.

A. Interaction between Statutes and Cases

After identifying the relevant portions of the statute, find cases relevant to that statute and use them to refine your understanding of the statute and its application to your facts. In the Medical Good Samaritan Immunity example, the legislature passed the law to address a matter of public concern: medical personnel being afraid to render emergency assistance because of the threat of tort liability. The legislature weighed the benefits of legal immunity, both for medical providers and members of the general public, against the risk that a particular individual or group of people might receive negligent care during an emergency. The legislature then struck a balance between the benefits and risk by creating a statute that continues to hold medical providers responsible for intentional or grossly negligent harm they might cause while providing them immunity from liability for all other acts or omissions they might commit while assisting at an emergency.

The law itself was drafted broadly so it would cover a wide variety of situations; however, the breadth of the law means that the definition of some terms in specific cases may have to be litigated. For example, whether a particular act or omission constituted "gross negligence" under Pennsylvania law would have to be resolved in court before a medical provider could claim immunity under the statute.

Another word that appears in some statutes that requires case-by-case analysis is "reasonable." In the Medical Good Samaritan Immunity example, a second subsection of the statute states that "good faith" includes a "reasonable belief" that care cannot be postponed until a victim is hospitalized. Thus, whether a medical provider reasonably believed that he or she had to perform a certain procedure outside of a hospital could be an issue that would have to be resolved before the provider could claim immunity under the statute.

When a dispute emerges over the application of a general statute to a specific situation, the court will look to previous cases interpreting the same statute to see how they defined and applied the disputed terms. If the statute has not previously been applied, the court may use other tools of legislative construction, such as looking at the application of closely related statutes or the statute's legislative history, to ascertain the legislature's intent.

Sometimes a statute codifies an existing common law principle. In this situation, previous cases will exist that did not consider the statute, even though they address an issue similar to the statutory issue you are researching. Whether these prior cases are relevant in interpreting the new statute will depend in large part on whether the statute closely tracks the prior common law principle or whether the statute was enacted to change some aspect of the common law principle. If a close comparison of the two reveals that the statutory language is very close to the common law principle, the cases applying the common law can still be cited as persuasive authority for how the statute, in turn, should be applied.

Other times, a statute may be enacted to overrule something a court has done. In such a situation, the older cases will not be binding, but they may provide insight into the legislature's intent.

B. Canons of Construction

Rules for interpreting statutes are sometimes called *canons of construction.* One of the most basic canons is that statutes should be interpreted according to their "plain meaning." In other words, courts should read the words of the statute, give them their ordinary meaning, and apply them to the facts of the case. Only when the words of a statute are ambiguous or would lead to absurd results if followed literally should courts refer to sources beyond the four corners of the statute. Some issues of statutory interpretation can be resolved without resorting to legislative history by using canons of construction.

There are a number of canons of construction, some of which appear to be contradictory. In fact, almost every rule of construction can be countered with another. For example, one court might interpret a statute according to the rule that "expressing one thing excludes another." Under this rule, the court might construe a statute that lists "trucks, cars, and motorcycles" to exclude scooters. Another court might interpret the same statute according to the rule that examples mentioned in a statute for purposes of illustration do not limit the statute's application; the second court might reason that "cars, trucks, and motorcycles" were illustrations of motorized vehicles and decide that the statute included a scooter equipped with a motor.[9] Although there are general similarities in these rules from one jurisdiction to the next, you should be familiar with the canons as they are most often applied in your jurisdiction.

C. Statutory Construction and the Use of Legislative History

In Pennsylvania, courts can consider legislative history to clarify ambiguous statutes.[10] Numerous cases emphasize that some ambiguity is necessary before

---

9. For a chart comparing 28 pairs of canons of construction, see Karl N. Llewellyn, *Remarks on the Theory of Appellate Decision and the Rules or Canons About How Statutes Are to be Construed,* 3 Vand. L. Rev. 395 (1950).

10. *See* 1 Pa. Cons. Stat. Ann. § 1921:

(a) The object of all interpretation and construction of statutes is to ascertain and effectuate the intention of the General Assembly. Every statute shall be construed, if possible, to give effect to all its provisions.

(b) When the words of a statute are clear and free from all ambiguity, the letter of it is not to be disregarded under the pretext of pursuing its spirit.

(c) When the words of the statute are not explicit, the intention of the General Assembly may be ascertained by considering, among other matters:

(1) The occasion and necessity for the statute.

(2) The circumstances under which it was enacted.

courts should consider anything other than the terms of the statute.[11] When you are writing a brief to a court, research the standards that court uses to decide whether to consult legislative history and frame your argument in terms of these standards. Another jurisdiction may use a slightly different vocabulary; it is your responsibility as an advocate to do the necessary research into the standards applied in each jurisdiction to enable you to present your client's case effectively.

Keep in mind that some courts are more receptive than others to arguments grounded in legislative history. Moreover, a court's approach to statutory construction can evolve over time. For example, in recent decades, the U.S. Supreme Court has demonstrated a shift from leaning heavily on legislative history to using it only in selected cases.[12]

Specific sources for legislative history research are discussed in greater detail in the next chapter.

---

(3) The mischief to be remedied.

(4) The object to be attained.

(5) The former law, if any, including other statutes upon the same or similar subjects.

(6) The consequences of a particular interpretation.

(7) The contemporaneous legislative history.

(8) Legislative and administrative interpretations of such statute.

11. *E.g.*, *Comm'r., Dep't of Transp. v. Taylor*, 576 Pa. 622, 628–29, 841 A.2d 108, 111–12 (2004).

12. *See generally* Stephen Breyer, *On the Uses of Legislative History in Interpreting Statutes*, 65 S. Cal. L. Rev. 845 (1992) (arguing against an abandonment of legislative history as an aid to construction). Justice Breyer identifies the following correct uses of legislative history, listed from the least to most controversial: clarifying ambiguity, avoiding absurd results, correcting drafting errors, taking account of specialized meanings given to certain terms, identifying the "reasonable purpose" underlying a particular term or provision, and choosing between different interpretations of a controversial statute. The article contains illustrations of each category drawn from his experience on the bench.

Chapter 4

Legislative History

Sometimes, although not always, you may need to research the history of legislation you are interpreting. Legislative history may prove useful if words of a statute are ambiguous or would lead to absurd results if followed literally.

The legislative history of a law is composed of the documents produced as proposed legislation—usually a bill—works its way through the process of becoming law. Examples of the documents that might be produced include committee reports, amended versions of bills, transcripts of hearings, and floor debates by legislators. The documents might include specific discussions of the purpose in enacting the law; discussions of what problem the law is intended to address; intention for using certain terminology; or the language of proposed amendments not been adopted, which might shed light on what the statute was not intended to do.

When the legislative history of a statute yields insight into the intent behind the statute, the legislative history can be used in court to try to persuade a judge to read the statutory language in a particular way.

This chapter begins with an overview of the basic legislative process for enacting a law. An explanation of Pennsylvania's legislative process is then covered, followed by how to find legislative history documents for Pennsylvania. This chapter concludes with an overview of how to conduct federal legislative history research.

I. Overview

The process of researching legislative history is similar across many jurisdictions, but there can be differences depending on the jurisdictional requirements for transcribing and publishing documents related to enactment of a bill. In general, far more sources for determining legislative intent exist at the federal level than at the state level.

The basic process followed by federal and state legislatures begins when a bill is drafted and introduced in one of the two chambers, or houses, of the legislature.[1] Next, the bill is assigned to a committee, which holds hearings on the bill, writes a report, and decides whether the bill will be tabled, amended, defeated, or accepted. If accepted, the reported bill goes to the chamber floor for debate. More amendments may be made once the bill is on the floor. After the debates on original and amended versions of the bill, the bill is voted on.

If the bill is passed by one chamber of the legislature, it is *engrossed*; it is then sent to the other chamber, where it goes through a similar process. If the second chamber amends and passes the bill, they ask the first chamber to *concur* with the new amendments. The first chamber then votes to either accept the amended version or reject it and request a conference. Representatives from both chambers are appointed to a *conference committee*. The committee meets to reconcile the differences in the two bill versions, votes on the reconciled version, and issues a report to both chambers. This report is not subject to amendment, and each chamber must either vote to accept or reject it as a whole. This report usually includes a joint statement by the conferees, which often is one of the best sources of legislative history. For this reason, the conference report is one of the most persuasive legislative history documents for federal laws.

Once the bill has passed both the House and the Senate, it is *enrolled* and sent to the executive (the President or Governor), who will either sign the bill into law, veto the bill, or do nothing. If the executive tables the bill, it may still become law after a certain number of days if the legislature is still in session. If the executive vetoes the bill, the legislature can override the executive with a specified proportion of votes from both chambers.

II. Pennsylvania Legislative History Research

Like the legislatures of most U.S. jurisdictions, Pennsylvania's General Assembly consists of two legislative chambers: the House of Representatives and the Senate. It is important to understand some unique steps in Pennsylvania's legislative process in order to know which documents are the most useful for ascertaining legislative intent and how to find those documents.

---

1. As of 2017, the state of Nebraska is the only state in the United States to have a unicameral legislature, meaning a legislature consisting of a single house. All other states have a bicameral legislature.

A. Pennsylvania Legislative Process

In Pennsylvania, legislators who want to sponsor a bill send their idea to the Legislative Reference Bureau (LRB), which writes the formal proposal and assigns a bill number based on the chamber in which the sponsors would like to introduce the bill (e.g., HB 1 or SB 1).[2] These bills are sometimes called *bluebacks*, referring to the color of the folder traditionally used for legislative proposals. The bill is then referred to a committee for discussion and either approval or rejection. Because of the volume of bills introduced in any given legislative session, the committee process is an extremely important part of the bill's development; most bills do not make it through this process to be voted on. The committee can hold a committee meeting on the bill; invite citizens, organizations, or experts to speak about the bill; hold public hearings; or create a subcommittee to study the bill further.

If the committee approves the bill, it is reported to the floor of the House or Senate. Before it is debated, possibly amended, and voted on, it goes through a caucus, a process where the two political parties discuss the bill privately with their members.

The Senate and House must both pass a bill before the bill is forwarded to the Governor for signature, but there are no requirements that a bill originate in one house or the other, with the exception of tax bills: the Pennsylvania Constitution requires that they originate in the House of Representatives. When the Senate and House pass different versions of a bill, the bill will be assigned to a conference committee to work out the differences. Sometimes a bill that originated in one chamber will be substituted for a similar bill in the other. Votes, floor amendments, committee action, and substitutions are all recorded in the daily *Journal of the Senate* and *Journal of the House of Representatives*.

When a bill is sent to the Governor, the Governor can sign it or can allow it to become law without a signature. If the Governor holds the bill for ten days during a legislative session or a month after the legislature adjourns, the bill becomes law without the Governor's approval. The Governor also has two veto options: a veto of the bill in its entirety or a line-item veto of spending portions of a bill. Any bills or specific provisions that are vetoed can be restored by a vote of two-thirds of the members of both chambers in the General Assembly. Once the bill has been enacted, it is given an *act number*.

Three main types of legislative documents are used for determining legislative intent in Pennsylvania. First are the amended versions of the bills, each of

---

2. The LRB website, www.palrb.net, provides access to session laws and other legislative history information.

which is assigned a unique *printer's number*. The different drafts of a bill indicate which provisions were added or deleted during the legislative process, so reviewing those different versions may be useful in determining legislative intent. Second are the *House* and *Senate Journals*, which contain the chamber debates and comments related to a bill. In Pennsylvania, journal remarks are the main source of legislative history. Third is the *pamphlet law*, which is the final version of the law. The pamphlet law, which is a session law, will sometimes include a preamble or other text stating the legislature's intent in creating the law.

Unlike federal legislative history, committee reports and hearing transcripts often are not very useful for ascertaining legislative intent, mainly because they are not widely available. When a committee report is available, it is usually brief and does not include much information about the committee's decision to support the bill. Because hearings are open to the public though, they are frequently covered in the press, and a search for news articles may yield some information about intent.

B. Locating Pennsylvania Legislative History

The first step in finding the history of an existing law (besides reading any legislative history information that appears in the annotated statutes) is to find which pamphlet law created the statute and which pamphlet laws, if any, subsequently amended it. This requires working back from the annotated statutes to *Laws of Pennsylvania*. Look at the history information at the end of the statute for a note like the following:

1976, July 9, P.L. 586, No. 142, § 2, effective June 27, 1978.

This note refers to a law that was enacted in 1976. The act number, No. 142, indicates that this was the 142nd law passed in 1976. In *Laws of Pennsylvania*, the pamphlet law appears at page 586. When the researcher consults *Laws of Pennsylvania*, the original bill number will be printed on the first page of the act.

With the bill number, you can consult the print History of House Bills and Resolutions, History of Senate Bills and Resolutions, or Combined History of Senate and House Bills. These print histories are arranged by bill number and will then direct you to the related *House* and *Senate Journal* entries for the debates and remarks, if there were any.

Because this law was passed after 1969, you could also bypass *Laws of Pennsylvania* and use the *Enacted Legislation* search feature on the General Assembly website to find the legislative history documents by year and act number. For example, you could search the 1976 database on the General Assembly website for Act No. 142 and learn that the original bill number was S.B. 935. Clicking the bill number would then take you to a page containing the bill's short title, the original sponsor, all the printer's numbers, and all the activity in the history of the bill. Sometimes also included in the history are links to committee reports (after 2007). Most important in the history though are the related *House* and *Senate Journal* remarks, which are sometimes hyperlinked directly to the journal entries. If the journal remarks are not hyperlinked, you simply retrieve the remarks from the corresponding chamber journals, which also are available on the General Assembly website, using the dates noted in the history.

If the law you are researching has been enacted fairly recently, you might be able to find relevant legislative history documents on Westlaw and Lexis Advance. These services have only limited legislative history documents, however. Westlaw directly links available legislative history documents to the statute itself on the *History* tab; on Lexis Advance, only the bills are directly linked to the statute. The General Assembly website provides access to far more documents for more years than Westlaw and Lexis Advance, and it is an open access website.

If you need to access older session laws, the LRB website and a service called HeinOnline provide coverage surpassing even the General Assembly website. The LRB has pamphlet laws online going back to 1960 (and a few years from the 1800s). Once on the LRB website, select *Browse* under the category *Pamphlet Laws* on the left. Then click *Go* after *view linked table of contents for a volume of the pamphlet laws by year*. Choose the applicable General Assembly by year. Find the correct page number (or act number) in General Laws. The *Session Laws Library* collection on HeinOnline includes the session laws for Pennsylvania going back to 1700. HeinOnline requires a subscription, but is available at many law and university libraries.

Jenkins Law Library in Philadelphia has a collection of already-compiled legislative histories for selected laws available online to its members. Non-members can view a list of the available histories in person and then order information on a fee basis.

In addition to these legislative materials, depending on the time and resources you have to allocate to your research project, you might also consider researching case decisions or secondary sources, including legal newspapers, discussing the statute. Sometimes a law review or bar journal article will contain information on concerns the legislature addressed when passing a particular bill.

III. Federal Legislative History Research

The United States Congress also consists of two legislative chambers, the House of Representatives and the Senate. Extensive information from both chambers is available online.

A. Federal Legislative Process

The federal legislative process basically follows the general outline described in the overview of this chapter.

Although the legislative process is similar to that of Pennsylvania, typically, more documents are generated throughout the federal legislative process. These documents are widely available online through a variety of paid and free re-search services. Different versions of a bill suggest changes that resulted from deliberations or compromise. Different versions of bills or amendments to bills also may be accompanied by remarks or prepared statements on the floor, which are published in the *Congressional Record*. The *Congressional Record* also includes the floor debates related to bills. During committee consideration, hearing transcripts, committee prints (background research, situational studies, legislative analyses, etc.), other miscellaneous documents ordered to be printed, and committee reports may be generated. A conference committee report also may be generated. Remember, a conference committee report is not created for every bill—a conference committee is created only if the two chambers initially pass different versions of the bill.

The persuasive value of the various legislative history documents at the fed-eral level also is different. Whereas in Pennsylvania you will likely look for the debates in the *House* and *Senate Journals*, conference committee reports and committee reports generally are considered the best evidence of federal leg-islative intent.

B. Locating Federal Legislative History

As with researching Pennsylvania legislative history, the most important piece of information you initially need to find is the public law number. Look at the history information at the end of the statute to see which public law created the statute and which public laws, if any, subsequently amended. For example:

Pub. L. 111-24, Title V, § 512, May 22, 2009, 123 Stat. 1764.

The public law number, Pub. L. 111-24, indicates this was the 24th law passed by the 111st Congress. You can use this public law number to find legislative history documents for this law through various services.

Legislative histories are often compiled for federal statutes; check for this before starting to research federal legislative history. Secondary sources, such as law review articles or other legal periodicals, may also be helpful starting points for researching a federal bill if the topic was of interest to scholars or practitioners. Some articles will provide lengthy discussions about the legislative history of particularly hot topics at the time. A useful source for beginning federal legislative history research is *Sources of Compiled Legislative Histories*, which is available on HeinOnline in the *U.S. Federal Legislative History Library* collection. Instead of linking directly to legislative history documents for a specific public law, this service links to articles detailing the legislative history for each public law included in the collection.

Congress.gov is the official website for federal legislative information. Administered by the Library of Congress, it provides open access to legislative materials. The documents are linked directly from the bills, which you can find using a bill number or public law number. From the *Actions* tab beneath the bill, you can access related *Congressional Record* entries, roll calls (votes), and committee reports. You can also access proposed amendments to the bill from using the *Amendments* tab, and all related bills using the *Related Bills* tab. The main limitations of Congress.gov are that not all legislative history documents, such as hearing transcripts, are linked, and coverage of materials generally only goes back to the mid-1990s. Given that it is free and user-friendly, though, this should be one of the first services you use.

Govinfo.gov, the website of the U.S. Government Publishing Office (GPO), provides open access to many authenticated government documents from all three branches. For purposes of legislative history, Govinfo.gov includes public and private laws dating back to the mid-1990s; the *Statutes at Large* dating back to the early 1950s; bills dating back to the early 1990s; and Congressional committee materials, including committee prints, hearings, and reports—all with varying coverage, but generally dating to the early 1990s. You can use the public law number to retrieve the PDF of the public law itself and a summary of legislative activity, which includes citations to reports and other related documents. Although the documents are not directly linked from the public law, you can access each document type separately using the citations.

Based on dates of coverage and types of legislative history documents available, ProQuest Congressional is the best service for researching federal legislative history. ProQuest Congressional is the online successor to the Congressional

Information Service (CIS), which was for many years the most comprehensive and thoroughly indexed source of federal legislative history information. You can search by bill number, public number, or *Statutes at Large* citation, and all available legislative documents will be retrieved, including bill texts, hearings, reports, *Congressional Record* entries, *Congressional Research Service* reports, and compiled legislative histories. Coverage of materials varies by type and the content subscription package, but some date back to the late 1800s. The main limitation to using ProQuest Congressional is that it is a paid service. However, some government law libraries and many university libraries provide on-site access to ProQuest Congressional. If you live or work near one of these institutions, a call to inquire if they are open to the public or members of the bar would be well worth your time.

Westlaw and Lexis Advance both provide access to legislative history documents, but coverage is limited and finding the documents can be a cumbersome process. Westlaw does a good job of linking available federal legislative history documents directly to the statute. On Westlaw, look for the *History* tab when viewing a statute to access previous versions of the statute, bill drafts, committee reports, *Congressional Record* entries, and other documents. Researching legislative history on Lexis Advance is not as straightforward, but you can view previous versions of the statute, view bill drafts using the bill tracking feature linked to each public law, and view the CIS legislative history linked to each public law. Westlaw and Lexis Advance each also include a *Legislative History* category for searching individual documents types, such as the *Congressional Record* and committee reports, or compiled legislative histories. The number of already compiled legislative histories on each platform is limited, but Westlaw's collection includes *Government Accountability Office Legislative Histories*, *United States Code Congressional and Administrative News Legislative Histories*, and *Arnold & Porter Legislative Histories*. Finally, Bloomberg Law provides access to a variety of legislative history documents, although its coverage is still less extensive than Westlaw or Lexis Advance.

If you are confronted with a project involving extensive federal legislative history research in practice and the online services do not meet your needs, consult law librarians or advanced legal research texts to locate other potential sources.

Chapter 5

Pennsylvania Constitutional Law

In general, constitutional issues arise when you are researching an issue that brings into question the scope of a governing body's authority or the appropriateness of some government action. For example, election law cases often raise constitutional law issues. Criminal law is another area where constitutional issues frequently arise. Depending on your area of practice, you may not need to research constitutional issues, or may research them only rarely. However, many areas of the law can intersect with constitutional law. For example, environmental issues may implicate property rights; family law issues may raise questions about whether a parent received due process. Thus, whenever you are researching an issue in which the state, or some branch of government, is one of the actors, you should think about whether the issue has constitutional implications.

I. The Pennsylvania Constitution[1]

The Commonwealth of Pennsylvania has had several constitutions since its first was enacted in 1776. The current constitution is the Constitution of 1874, although it was largely updated and rewritten following a constitutional convention in 1967–1968. Some portions have been amended since 1968, as well.

The Constitution of 1776 and its successor, the Constitution of 1790, could only be amended through a convention process. The Constitution of 1838 created a process of allowing constitutional amendments by the legislature. Under this process, the constitution could be amended if the Pennsylvania General Assembly passed an amendment in two consecutive sessions and the amendment was then ratified by the electorate. This amendment process was main-

---

1. A much more detailed history than that provided here is available on the website of the Pennsylvania Bar Constitutional Revision Commission, www.pabarcrc.org/history.asp.

tained in the Constitution of 1874, as well as in the revisions of 1968, and is in effect today. Amendments to a constitutional provision cannot be submitted to the electorate for ratification more than once in any five-year period. Other than that, and the need for the proposed amendments to pass in the state Senate and House of Representatives for two consecutive sessions, there is no limit on how often the constitution can be amended.

II. Finding a Pennsylvania Constitutional Provision and Cases Interpreting It

The Pennsylvania Constitution is published in *Purdon's Pennsylvania Statutes and Consolidated Statutes Annotated*, so the process of locating a specific provision and cases interpreting it is very much like the process of locating statutory provisions, whether in print or online. Begin by identifying research terms, and then search for relevant constitutional provisions. Once you have located those provisions, read them and look for notes of decisions listing cases that have interpreted or applied those provisions. The annotations following each provision will direct you to other research sources, as well.

The constitution itself, without annotations, is also widely available on a number of websites.[2] It can also be searched in either annotated or unannotated statutory databases on Westlaw and Lexis Advance.

For historical research, previous versions of the constitution are available both online and in print. Debates and reports of constitutional conventions from 1967–1968 and earlier are also available in bound volumes and online.

Research in secondary sources, particularly journal articles, can be helpful in determining whether your issue raises constitutional questions. You can then use key word searching within the constitution itself, or simply browse the index, to locate and read the applicable constitutional provisions. Always base your analysis on the text of the provisions, just as you would with a statute. Although it is unlikely that any particular constitutional provision has changed, because amendments require such a lengthy process, you should check to be

---

2. The constitution is published in the *Pennsylvania Manual*, a guide to state government published by the Pennsylvania Department of General Services, Bureau of Publications, which is available at www.dgs.pa.gov. Another place to locate the current constitution is the Pennsylvania Constitution Web Page of the Duquesne University School of Law, www.duq.edu/academics/gumberg-library/pa-constitution. The website has links to summaries of court decisions, copies of earlier versions of the constitution, and various other research sources.

sure you are looking at a current version of the constitution as well. In the annotated codes, whether in print or online, the annotations themselves will tell you when, if ever, your provision has been amended.

III. Researching Other Constitutions

Most state constitutions are published, and can be researched, in the same way as a particular state's annotated statutes.

Different states amend their constitutions with different frequencies, and also have a variety of mechanisms for proposing and approving amendments. In most states, amendments to the state constitution can be developed through a constitutional convention, or proposed by the legislature, and have to be approved by a majority of voters. In about one-third of states, a ballot initiative—a proposed law that does not come through the legislature—can also be used to amend the state constitution. It is essential that you consult a reference text specific to the jurisdiction whose constitution you are researching for additional guidance on locating, updating and interpreting that jurisdiction's constitutional provisions.

If you need to research the federal constitution, you will find that secondary sources are particularly helpful. The federal constitution is broad and many doctrines emanating from its provisions—such as the right of privacy—are not specifically mentioned there. The amendment process is lengthy and seldom used, in comparison with state processes; the last amendment to the federal constitution added the 27th Amendment (relating to changes in Congressional salaries) in 1992. Therefore, much of federal constitutional law has developed through court decisions rather than through the amendment process. Referring to a treatise on constitutional law (either a broad one or a treatise that emphasizes one aspect of constitutional law, such as a treatise devoted solely to search and seizure) will help you narrow your search for applicable cases and may reveal recognized "landmark" cases without which your research will be incomplete. The text of the U.S. Constitution is published in both sets of annotated federal statutes, and is also available on a number of websites.

When researching constitutional law, be attentive to distinctions between the state and federal constitutions. Although there is often overlap between the two, they are not identical. State constitutions can give greater protection to state citizens than the federal constitution does. For example, Pennsylvania's Constitution contains the following provision: *Equality of rights under the law shall not be denied or abridged in the Commonwealth of Pennsylvania because of the sex of the individual.*[3] A similar amendment to the federal constitution has been attempted, but has never succeeded. The Pennsylvania Constitution also allows the General Assembly to authorize verdicts by a five-sixths vote in civil cases, rather than requiring unanimity.[4] The federal constitution does not have that level of specificity.

Because of these distinctions, a researcher cannot assume that cases or commentary discussing a federal constitutional doctrine are equally applicable to the Pennsylvania Constitution. In any situation where you need to research both state and federal constitutional provisions, keep your research sources and notes separate, so that your analysis of state and federal constitutional law is clear.

---

3. Pa. Const. Art. I, § 28.
4. Pa. Const. Art. I, § 6.

Chapter 6

Administrative Law

Many beginning legal researchers make the mistake of believing that complete research can be done using only the primary legal materials produced by the legislative and judicial branches. This is a significant and costly omission, however, as such an approach leaves out the law produced by the third branch of government—the executive branch. This body of law is known as administrative law.

I. What Is Administrative Law?

Administrative law includes the issuances of the executive, such as the President at the national level and the Governor at the state level, as well as the regulatory activities and actions of agencies. Agencies are government organizations that are responsible for the day-to-day enforcement and administration of federal and state laws in specific areas, and their directors are typically selected by presidential or gubernatorial appointment. Examples of agencies in Pennsylvania include the Department of Environmental Protection, the Department of Aging, and the Department of Transportation.

The primary regulatory activity of agencies is the promulgation of regulations, which typically provide more detailed explanations of the requirements of a statute. Administrative regulations build on the intention behind the statutory enactments, setting forth the detailed rules and procedures needed for the laws to function effectively, and they exist at both the state and federal levels. In addition to regulations and executive orders, administrative law also includes administrative decisions, which are opinions by administrative law judges.

There are two critical points to remember when researching administrative law. The first is that regulations have the same force of law as any other primary legal material, such as statutes and case law. The second is that agencies do not have the power to create regulations on their own. Instead, they may only create regulations in response to specific authority delegated by the legislature. This is called enabling legislation. This delegation of authority limits the power an agency may use in accomplishing its goals, but it also allows the legislature, which is composed of generalists, to transfer lawmaking responsibility in these areas to agencies with more specialized knowledge of an area.

II. The Administrative Lawmaking Process

The "Administrative Law and Procedure" title of the Pennsylvania statutes provides that "an agency shall have power to promulgate, amend and repeal reasonable regulations implementing the provisions of this title."[1] Unlike the federal government and many other states, however, Pennsylvania does not mandate a uniform procedure for doing so. As a result, most agencies in Pennsylvania have adopted their own procedural rules for creating implementing regulations.

In contrast, the federal government has a very specific set of procedures agencies must follow in promulgating regulations. These procedural steps are set forth in the Administrative Procedure Act,[2] and they are:

Step 1: Enabling Legislation. The legislature delegates authority to an agency to promulgate one or more regulations in furtherance of a legislative enactment. The legislative body selects the agency based on its subject matter expertise. Agency staff members then draft regulations consistent with this authority.

Step 2: New Regulations Proposed. The agency publishes its proposed regulations in an official government publication. At the federal level, this publication is called the *Federal Register*. The closest equivalent in Pennsylvania is the *Pennsylvania Bulletin*.

Step 3: Notice and Comment Period. Interested parties have an opportunity to review the new regulations and submit comments on them as part of a notice and comment period. Anyone can comment, including other government entities, private entities, and private individuals. The notice and comment period typically runs for thirty to sixty days, but it can run longer for especially complicated regulations. The agency may also hold hearings on the proposed regulations during this period.

---

1. 2 Pa.C.S. § 102(a).
2. 5 U.S.C. § 551 et seq.

Step 4: Consideration of Comments. The agency staff reviews the comments it received, as well as any hearing testimony, and then considers whether to make changes to the proposed regulations. In most cases the agency makes at least minimal changes to the proposed regulations, but the agency may make substantial changes based on this feedback. This step of the process can take a significant amount of time, depending on the volume of comments on a given set of regulations.

Step 5: Final Regulations Published. The agency finalizes its regulations and publishes them in the same publication where it published its proposed regulations. This is called a "final rule," and it includes a great deal of explanatory information as well as reproducing the final version of the regulations. Again, the final rules are published in the *Federal Register* at the federal level, and the *Pennsylvania Bulletin* is the closest equivalent in Pennsylvania.

Step 6: Regulations Compiled by Subject. The final regulations are added to an administrative code, which is organized by subject and only includes the regulations that are currently in effect. At the federal level, this publication is called the *Code of Federal Regulations*. In Pennsylvania, this publication is called the *Pennsylvania Code*.

Once this process is complete and the final regulations are in place, the regulations are legally binding on all individuals or entities within the jurisdictions where the agency operates. Going forward, the rules may allow or require an agency to conduct public hearings from time to time to seek additional public input or evaluate how agency programs are working. The rules may also include a right to a hearing before an administrative law judge. These hearings are considered quasi-judicial proceedings because they often involve the same types of pleadings, briefs, witnesses, arguments, and written decisions as traditional judicial proceedings.

III. Pennsylvania Administrative Law Research

A. Sources of Pennsylvania Administrative Law

The two primary sources for researching administrative law in Pennsylvania are the *Pennsylvania Bulletin* and the *Pennsylvania Code*.

The *Pennsylvania Bulletin* is the official gazette for administrative information within the Commonwealth, and it includes proposed and approved changes to state agency regulations. It also publishes agency notices, information on state contracts and bid opportunities, statewide and local court rules, and Proclamations and Executive Orders of the Governor. The *Pennsylvania Bulletin* is published weekly, and it is only available in an electronic format, although historical copies may still exist in print.[3] The site has full-text and field search capabilities, as well as find by citation and browsing options. In addition, the *Pennsylvania Bulletin* is available in commercial databases, including Westlaw, Lexis Advance, and Bloomberg Law.

The *Pennsylvania Code* is the official compilation of administrative regulations. Organized by subject, it includes all of the regulations that are currently in effect in Pennsylvania. Following the text of the regulation itself, a source note tells researchers the history of each regulation, including when it was enacted, when it was amended, and what enabling legislation authorized its creation or amendment. The *Pennsylvania Code* is available in both print and electronic formats. The site has full-text search capabilities as well as the ability to browse by title. The *Pennsylvania Code* is also available in commercial databases, including Lexis Advance, Westlaw, and Bloomberg Law.

B. Researching Pennsylvania Administrative Law

Most administrative law research should begin with the *Pennsylvania Code*, as it has the regulations that are currently in effect in Pennsylvania. Even if you plan to use the *Pennsylvania Bulletin* at some point in your research, it is almost always best to start in the administrative code, as you can find citations to the key portions of the *Pennsylvania Bulletin* from the code. Trying to search the *Pennsylvania Bulletin* on its own is usually an exercise in frustration.

The next step is choosing a research method. The one you choose will depend on what you already know. If you have a known citation to one or more regulations from your prior research, which is especially likely if you started your research using one or more secondary sources, locate the relevant regulation using its citation. Most platforms have a "find by citation" feature, and the citation is also a field/segment in Westlaw and Lexis Advance.

If you have a known statute instead, and you are using an annotated code, start by looking for references to regulations within the annotations for the statute you found. You may also find these connections using a citator (KeyCite or Shepard's). If this fails, then use terms and connectors or natural language searching with terms generated from your statutory research. In addition, there may be specialized tools for finding regulations based on a known statute. See the later section on finding federal administrative law for more information on these tools.

---

3. The Commonwealth posts a current version online at www.pabulletin.com, as well as historical versions dating back to 1996.

If you do not have a citation to a regulation or statute, you must search by topic or agency name. Begin by looking to see if there is an index available. Currently, there is no online index for the *Pennsylvania Code*, but this may change with time. Browsing the titles and chapter headings is a good option because administrative codes are organized by subject, and the number of regulations is usually more manageable at the state level. Finally, terms and connectors and natural language can be very effective here as well. Remember to spend the necessary time to plan a smart search, including generating synonyms and word variants. This is important whether you are using terms and connectors or natural language searching.

Note there are additional tools to help you search for regulations in the *Pennsylvania Code* if you are doing print research. For example, if you have a known statute, you can access the Table of Authorities and look up your statute, and it will direct you to cross-referenced regulations. Once you locate a title on point, you can use the subject matter index that appears at the end of each title to find more relevant regulations. If you know the agency that promulgated the regulation you are researching, there is an Alphabetical Index of Agencies, which points you to the title containing regulations from that agency.

Once you have one or more relevant regulations, continue your research in this area by reviewing relevant sections in the *Pennsylvania Bulletin* and relevant case law, including both traditional case law and administrative law decisions (covered later in this chapter). Your research should also include finding and reviewing the appropriate enabling legislation, especially if there is any doubt about whether an agency acted within its authority provided by the legislature.

C. Updating Pennsylvania Regulations

Once you find relevant regulations, you will need to make sure there have not been any recent changes to them. Start by determining how up-to-date the regulations are. This is true whether you are using an electronic version or a print version. In Westlaw, Lexis Advance, or Bloomberg Law, look for a reference to the currentness of the regulation. (Do not confuse this with the copyright date at the bottom of the screen.) Then, use a citator to check for pending or newly approved changes.

Going forward, to ensure you learn of new changes as quickly as possible, you should use the tracking tools available online. Westlaw has a "Pennsylvania Regulation Tracking" database, and Lexis Advance has a "PA State Regulation

Tracking" database. In addition, you can set up search alerts to run at regular intervals and notify you of any changes in Westlaw, Lexis Advance, and Bloomberg Law.

If you are doing research in another online platform or a print resource, your process will be slightly different. For whatever version of the code you are using, find the date it was last updated. The online versions will typically reference how current the code is; the first binder in the print version of the *Pennsylvania Code* provides information on when pages in the binders were last updated in particular titles. Once you have this information, you must check any issues of the *Pennsylvania Bulletin* published after that date for references to your regulation. If you access the Pennsylvania Code Chapters Affected section within each issue, it will reference any recent or proposed changes to your regulation.

D. Historical Research

Some research projects require finding the text of a regulation no longer in force. It may be newly out of date or it may have been in force many years ago. The source note following each regulation in the *Pennsylvania Code* will let you know if a regulation has been changed and when the change occurred.

The next step in historical regulatory research is to find the older version of the regulation. If you can find this through an online resource, you are highly encouraged to do so. Westlaw, for example, has historical versions of the *Pennsylvania Code* back to 2002. There are also historical versions of the *Pennsylvania Bulletin* online, as noted above, but trying to cobble together the information yourself using the register is much more complicated, time-consuming, and prone to overlooked information or other error than using historical versions of the code.

If the regulation you need predates what you can find online, you should consider reaching out to a law librarian for help, as finding historical regulations in print is a more complicated process. The easiest way to do so is to try to find a local law library that retains earlier editions of the *Pennsylvania Code*. Next best is to use the Pages by Sequential Serial Number finding aid. Each page of the *Pennsylvania Code* has a serial number designed to aid in updating it in print, and these serial numbers allow you to locate prior versions in the superseded pages. Unfortunately, the collected Pages by Sequential Serial Number are published in very limited quantities, and only specialized law libraries have them. In lieu of these pages, some libraries maintain unofficial sets of superseded pages or older copies of the *Pennsylvania Bulletin* to aid in historical research. Again, ask for help if you are doing this type of research.

IV. Federal Administrative Law Research

State and federal administrative law research have a great deal in common. The publication names are different, but the federal level has a register (*Federal Register*) and a code (*Code of Federal Regulations*) just like Pennsylvania. Beyond the uniformity in the process for creating regulations at the federal level, which does not exist in Pennsylvania, the main differences in federal administrative law research are the availability of additional tools for finding relevant regulations at the federal level, and the ease in finding online access to historical versions of both the register and the code dating back to their inception in the 1930s.

A. Sources of Federal Administrative Law

1. Code of Federal Regulations

The *Code of Federal Regulations* (CFR) is the official compilation of federal regulations currently in effect. It is divided into 50 titles, which are arranged by subject matter. Note that these titles may, but do not always, correspond to the same subject matter in the U.S. Code. In addition to the text of the regulations, the CFR includes authority notes and source notes, which cite to the enabling legislation for each regulation and reference the changes to each regulation over time.

The Government Publishing Office (GPO) publishes the official version of the CFR online through its "govinfo" website,[4] which allows you to browse the contents of each title or search using either basic or advanced search tools. Historical versions of the CFR are available starting in 1996.

The CFR is updated once per year on a quarterly publication schedule, which mirrors the print publication schedule, but users can update regulations using the e-CFR at ecfr.gpo.gov. While unofficial, the e-CFR is the most up-to-date version of the CFR online, including both free websites and commercial platforms. Individual agency sites often include links to the regulations promulgated by that agency as well.

---

4. Prior names for this site, www.govinfo.gov, include GPO's Federal Digital System (FDsys) and GPO Access.

The CFR is also available through a series of commercial databases. Westlaw, Lexis Advance, and Bloomberg Law all include current and historical versions of the CFR, and HeinOnline has a full run of the CFR dating back to its inception in 1938. These databases are more up-to-date than the official version of the CFR, they have stronger coverage, and they offer additional research enhancements and connections between relevant materials.

2. Federal Register

The *Federal Register* ("FR") is published every weekday, and it lists recent agency actions and proposed actions. These actions include the notices, proposed rules, and final rules produced as part of the rulemaking process discussed above, as well as descriptions of agency organization and reorganization. Final rules in particular contain a wealth of information not available anywhere else, including detailed explanations of why the rules were written as they were. The FR also includes information no longer found in the CFR, such as rules that have been repealed, so the FR is critical for any historical regulatory research.

Like the CFR, the official version of the FR is available online through GPO's "govinfo" website, and coverage dates back to 1994. Due to the sheer volume of the FR, which numbers hundreds of thousands of pages per year, searching using a known citation is the best search option. Basic and advanced searching by keyword is available as well.

Like the CFR, the FR is also available through a series of commercial databases. Westlaw, Lexis Advance, and Bloomberg Law have current and historical coverage, and HeinOnline has the complete FR dating back to 1936.

B. Researching Federal Administrative Law

Many of the tools for researching federal administrative law are the same tools outlined in the state section above or they provide a similar version of a given tool. One example is the Parallel Table of Authorities & Rules in the official index to the CFR, which serves much the same function as the Table of Authorities in Pennsylvania. However, it is important to note that commercial databases provide enhanced searching capabilities at the federal level. For example, both Westlaw and Lexis Advance have detailed cross-references to relevant regulations, either in their statutory annotations or via their citators (Shepard's or KeyCite), and the regulations themselves are heavily annotated in both platforms. In addition, Westlaw has a detailed index to the CFR, which provides one of the most precise and effective entry points to federal regulations, and the "authority" field/segment on both platforms allows you to search using a statutory citation to find relevant regulations based on their enabling legislation.

C. Updating Federal Administrative Regulations

As noted above, the easiest way to update the CFR is via GPO's unofficial e-CFR website. It is the most up-to-date version of the CFR online, including both free websites and commercial platforms, and it is very easy to use. In addition, commercial platforms update the CFR regularly, including Westlaw, Lexis Advance, and Bloomberg Law. When using the CFR through any online platform, be sure to check how current it is. If you are researching a hot topic or expect regulatory changes any day, the only way to do a complete update of the CFR is to check the "current through" date on the online platform and then review the FR for each day between that date and the date of your review.

This process may sound laborious, but it is far less so than updating the CFR in print. The CFR is published on a quarterly basis in print, and each volume of the CFR is only published once per year. This leaves a significant amount of time for the CFR to become out of date. To make updating easier, GPO publishes a monthly booklet called the List of Sections Affected ("LSA"). It is available in print and online through GPO's "govinfo" website. The LSA lists the sections of any regulations changed within that month and all preceding months since the CFR was last updated. Therefore, to update a regulation from the CFR in print, you must review every LSA between the date your provision was last published and today. Once you exhaust the LSAs, you must review the FR for each day between the date of the last available LSA and the date of your review. Again, it is a laborious process. You are strongly encouraged to update your regulations using an online source instead.

D. Historical Federal Research

Historical research is much easier at the federal level than it is in Pennsylvania. As noted above, HeinOnline has a full set of the CFR and the FR, dating back to 1938 and 1936 respectively. The easiest way to do this research is to access and review older versions of the CFR so you can track changes over time, and then you should retrieve and review relevant portions of the FR by citation as appropriate. The credits field following the regulation will let you know when changes have been made, so you can use that information to target the years of greatest use. If the historical version of the CFR is recent enough, other online sources like GPO's "govinfo" website, as well as commercial platforms like Westlaw and Lexis Advance provide access.

V. Administrative Agency Decisions

The focus of this chapter has been on the role of administrative agencies in promulgating regulations, but agencies can also have quasi-judicial roles that allow them to adjudicate cases on agency rules and regulations. Most Pennsylvania agencies do not publish these decisions, and there is no general publication covering them. Unpublished adjudications may be available directly from the agency, but sometimes they are only made available to the parties involved. Appeals from certain agency decisions are heard in the Commonwealth Court and reported in the *Atlantic Reporter*.[5]

Examples of administrative law agencies that issue decisions in Pennsylvania include the Pennsylvania Environmental Hearing Board, the Pennsylvania Public Utilities Commission, the Pennsylvania Securities Commission, and the Pennsylvania Workers Compensation Appeals Board. These opinions are available on the agency's website as well as through commercial databases like Westlaw and Lexis Advance. This is not an exhaustive list, however. If you are interested in the work of another state agency, check its website to see if they issue opinions and if they make them available.

Note also that a Pennsylvania agency can issue a "Statement of Policy" regarding a particular issue or the agency's broader role. These statements are advisory, not binding, but are often highly persuasive. They include an agency's interpretation of specific rules. Statements of Policy go through the same notice and comment process that a regulation goes through, and are published in the *Pennsylvania Bulletin*. Final Statements of Policy are published in the *Pennsylvania Code*.

In many states, opinions of the state Attorney General are a potential source of information when a researcher needs to analyze the interpretation or implementation of a particular statute by an administrative agency. Researching an issue involving some challenge to an agency action or determination may require determining whether the Attorney General has issued an advisory opinion on point. These advisory opinions are fairly rare in Pennsylvania, however, so they are used less frequently in Pennsylvania than in other jurisdictions. These opinions are available through the Pennsylvania Office of the Attorney General[6] as well as through commercial databases and older print volumes.

---

5. These decisions were published in *Pennsylvania Commonwealth Court Reports* until 1995, and you may still see references to that reporter in older print materials.

6. The website is www.attorneygeneral.gov/The_Office/Official_Attorney_General_Opinions/.

At the federal level, some federal agencies publish their own reporters for agency decisions, and unofficial reports cover other agency decisions.[7] In addition, an agency's website will often provide information about where to find that agency's decisions. For a detailed list of access points for federal agency decisions, see the "Administrative Decisions" research guide by the University of Virginia Libraries.[8] Westlaw and Lexis Advance also have administrative law databases containing federal agency decisions, and legal looseleafs may reproduce some of these decisions as well. Legal looseleafs are discussed in much greater detail in the chapter on practice materials.

VI. Executive Issuances

There are a variety of executive issuances at both the state and federal levels, but executive orders are by far the most prominent among them and the most useful for most legal research needs.

Both the Governor of Pennsylvania and the President of the United States use executive orders to direct and manage the operations of executive agencies and officers. They have the full force of law if derived from the proper authority. Pennsylvania's Office of Administration makes selected executive orders available back to 1973, and they are also available in the *Pennsylvania Bulletin*.[9] Federal executive orders are available on the website of the White House, as well as in sources such as the *Daily Compilation of Presidential Documents*, the *Federal Register*, and Title 3 of the *Code of Federal Regulations*.[10] Federal executive orders are also available using commercial databases.

VII. Oversight of Administrative Agencies

One last "big picture" point about administrative law research is that researching these issues requires an understanding of not only how agencies work, but also the relationship between agencies and other branches of government. The legislature, executive branch, and judiciary each have special roles in overseeing administrative agencies. Be sure to keep these in mind when researching administrative law issues.

---

7. For a list of agency reporters, see Table 1.2 in *The Bluebook: A Uniform System of Citation* (20th ed. 2015).
8. The guide is available at http://guides.lib.virginia.edu/administrative_decisions.
9. The website is op.pa.gov.
10. The website for the White House is www.whitehouse.gov.

The legislature can oversee agencies in a number of ways. Legislatures will sometimes hold oversight hearings to examine whether an agency is properly performing its job. Legislatures also control the funding of agencies, and a legislature may cut funding to an agency or even eliminate an agency altogether if it disagrees with the agency's action or wants to diminish its impact. In addition, the legislature can pass new statutory law in response to the agency's action, which in turn may expand or limit the scope of the agency's responsibility. Finally, in many jurisdictions, the legislature must approve the executive's appointment of top agency officials.

The executive branch also plays an important role in agency administration. Most obviously, the executive typically appoints an agency's top official or officials. Depending on the jurisdiction and the agency, the executive might be able to appoint or remove an agency head at any time, or may be limited to removing that official for cause. Some agency officials are elected as well. The agency's top official may be part of the executive's cabinet or some other advisory group. In Pennsylvania, the Cabinet includes the top officials of a number of agencies. They are appointed by the Governor, but also go through a confirmation process in the Pennsylvania Senate.

The judicial branch also has an important role in overseeing agency action. If an agency action is challenged in court, the court will review the action to determine whether it was within the agency's power, as defined by the enabling statute. The constitutionality of a rule itself, or whether the rule is within the scope of the agency's mandate, is another legal issue that can be raised and decided in court. A court can also review whether the agency used the proper procedures in taking an action. In some limited circumstances, parties who receive an adverse ruling in a quasi-judicial agency proceeding will have a right of appeal to the courts.

Chapter 7

Rules of Court and Ethics

For many attorneys, the most familiar court rules are procedural rules. Those rules govern such things as which parties may be joined in a civil action, when summary judgment is appropriate, when a party can appeal an unfavorable decision, and what grounds will justify imposing sanctions on attorneys. Other court rules govern more mundane aspects of litigation, such as filing procedures, payment of fees, and mandatory pre-trial conferences. Whenever beginning work on a litigation matter, an attorney should determine which rules of court apply. In addition, through rules of professional conduct, courts regulate the comportment of attorneys in the practice of law. These rules address the relationships of attorneys with clients, opposing counsel, the court, and others.

I. Overview

Court rules govern all aspects of court proceedings, whether the context is civil, criminal, or appellate. Each state has its own rules of procedure. While these state rules are frequently similar to the federal rules and to the rules of other states, you must research the rules governing the court with jurisdiction over your case. Do not assume that your state's rule is exactly the same as the federal rule or the rule of a state in which you previously litigated. For example, if you were drafting a motion for summary judgment to be filed in a Pennsylvania state court, you would need to research Rules 1035.1 through 1035.5 of the Pennsylvania Rules of Civil Procedure, not Rule 56 of the Federal Rules of Civil Procedure.

Adopting and revising the rules governing court systems are tasks generally delegated to the highest court in a jurisdiction. When that court adopts a rule or revises the language in an existing rule, the resulting rule applies throughout the jurisdiction. In addition, however, individual courts can adopt local rules that supplement the general rules of the jurisdiction. For example, Federal

Rule of Civil Procedure 16 sets out pretrial procedures that are required in all federal district courts. In the Eastern District of Pennsylvania, Local Civil Rule 16.1(b) requires, as part of these pretrial procedures, that a scheduling conference be held by the assigned judge or magistrate within 120 days after the filing of a complaint. In the Western District of Pennsylvania, however, Local Civil Rule 16.1.A.2 requires a scheduling conference to be held within 90 days of when any defendant is served, or within 60 days of when any defendant enters an appearance, whichever is earlier.

Court rules cannot conflict with statutes, or give parties greater or fewer rights than are available under applicable substantive law.[1] Even with that limitation, court rules can often affect the availability of a substantive remedy, and court rules have the force of law within the jurisdiction where the rule is promulgated.

II. Researching Pennsylvania Rules of Court

Article V, section 10(c) of the Pennsylvania Constitution gives the Pennsylvania Supreme Court authority to prescribe general rules governing practice, procedure, and the conduct of all Pennsylvania courts, including administration of all courts and supervision of all officers of the Judicial Branch. In addition, the Pennsylvania Supreme Court has the power to set forth standards for admission to the bar and to practice law. Pennsylvania has rules of court for many areas, including the following:

- Pennsylvania Rules of Civil Procedure
- Pennsylvania Rules of Appellate Procedure
- Pennsylvania Rules of Criminal Procedure
- Pennsylvania Rules of Evidence
- Pennsylvania Rules of Judicial Administration
- Pennsylvania Code of Judicial Conduct
- Pennsylvania Bar Admission Rules
- Pennsylvania Rules of Professional Conduct
- Pennsylvania Rules of Disciplinary Enforcement.

A. Finding the Text of Pennsylvania Rules of Court

Pennsylvania court rules are published in many different formats. Often, court rules are included in statutory compilations as a service to attorneys.

---

1. *See* 28 U.S.C. § 2072 (2012).

(Remember, however, that court rules are not statutes.) *Purdon's Pennsylvania Statutes and Consolidated Statutes Annotated* publishes Pennsylvania Rules of Court within Title 42. You can use the detailed Table of Contents at the beginning of each set of rules to locate a specific rule on point. The official compilation, *Pennsylvania Consolidated Statutes*, does not include court rules.

In addition, the *Pennsylvania Code* publishes certain Pennsylvania rules, including the Pennsylvania Rules of Judicial Administration (Title 201), the Pennsylvania Rules of Appellate Procedure (Title 210), and the Pennsylvania Rules of Civil Procedure (Title 231), among others. Pennsylvania rules of court procedure and evidence may be accessed via the website for the Pennsylvania Code, at www.pacode.com. Pennsylvania Code online includes notes from the drafters, but no case annotations. To find the text of the rules, click on "Browse" and scroll down to the bottom of the list, where you will see the rules listed under Title 210 — Appellate Court Procedural Rules, through Title 246 — Minor Court Rules. The Pennsylvania Code online also includes a search function.

Court rules are also available in *deskbooks*. These are soft-cover collections of the rules of a particular jurisdiction, making deskbooks compact sources for the text of rules. Deskbooks also usually include some of the notes from the drafters of the rules, but no case annotations. West publishes a deskbook for each state with rules of court for that state. *Pennsylvania Rules of Court: Volume I — State* contains all the sets of rules mentioned above and some lesser-known rules. Moreover, PBI (the Pennsylvania Bar Institute) Press publishes both *The Pennsylvania Rules of Evidence with Commentary* and a pocket edition of the *Pennsylvania Rules of Evidence* without commentary.

Local Pennsylvania court rules are available through Westlaw by searching in the "Pennsylvania Statutes and Court Rules" database, via Lexis Advance by searching in the "PA — Pennsylvania Local, State & Federal Court Rules" database, and via Bloomberg Law in the "Pennsylvania Court Rules" database. They are also often posted on the websites of individual courts.

B. Interpreting Specific Pennsylvania Rules of Court

Usually, finding a rule of court that addresses an issue is just the beginning of the research process. To fully understand Pennsylvania court rules, a researcher must read Pennsylvania case law. Many sources provide citations to case law and commentary interpreting Pennsylvania rules of court. As noted above, *Purdon's Pennsylvania Statutes and Consolidated Statutes Annotated* includes rules of court, along with historical notes, committee notes, cross-references to related statutes and rules, citations to law review articles, library references, and annotations to case law. Another way to find cases interpreting Pennsylvania rules is to research in a commercial database. For example, in Westlaw, you may find cases interpreting the Pennsylvania Rules of Civil Procedure by reviewing the "Notes of Decisions" for a specific rule. Similarly, review the "Case Notes" in Lexis Advance to find case law interpreting individual Pennsylvania court rules.

Treatises are often helpful sources for material interpreting court rules. For an in-depth analysis of the Pennsylvania rules, consult a treatise such as *Ohlbaum on the Pennsylvania Rules of Evidence*, which is published by Lexis in print, and is also available via Lexis Advance. The Ohlbaum treatise contains the complete text of the Pennsylvania Rules of Evidence, official commentary by the rule drafters, case notes and commentary by the Honorable Daniel J. Anders, General Editor, comparisons with the Federal Rules of Evidence, and cross-references to related Pennsylvania statutes and rules. Other helpful Pennsylvania treatises include *Standard Pennsylvania Practice* and *Goodrich-Amram 2d Procedural Rules Service with Forms*, both of which are published by West and accessible via Westlaw. These sources are useful because they contain not only the rules, but also accompanying forms.

C. Finding Amendments to Pennsylvania Rules of Court

Amendments to Pennsylvania court rules are first published in the *Pennsylvania Bulletin*.[2] When the Pennsylvania Supreme Court amends a rule or adopts a new rule, the order and rule text are posted on the "Court Opinions and Postings" webpage.[3] The "Court Opinions and Postings" database contains postings dating from 1997; it is searchable and updated daily with new orders and opinions. Proposed and updated rules are also available via the webpages for the seven procedural rules committees established by the Pennsylvania Supreme Court.[4] New and proposed rules are also posted on Twitter via the handle @SCO-PARules. New rules are also published in *Purdon's Legislative Service* pamphlets.

III. Researching Federal Rules of Court

Although Congress has the power to make rules of procedure for the federal courts, it delegated rulemaking authority to the United States Supreme Court

---

2. The *Pennsylvania Bulletin* is available online at www.pabulletin.com.

3. Orders adopting or amending rules are available at www.pacourts.us/courts/supreme-court/court-opinions/.

4. The Rules Committee webpage, at www.pacourts.us/courts/supreme-court/committees/rules-committees, has links for specific procedural committees.

in the Rules Enabling Act of 1934. The Supreme Court first adopted the Federal Rules of Civil Procedure in 1938. The Federal Rules of Civil Procedure apply to cases litigated in federal district courts. Federal Rule of Civil Procedure 83 allows each district court to promulgate its own local rules, so long as those rules are consistent with (but do not duplicate) federal statutes and rules adopted under 28 U.S.C. §§ 2072 and 2075. A similar combination of rules applies to cases at the appellate level. The Federal Rules of Appellate Procedure apply to all federal circuits; each circuit has its own local rules as well as internal operating procedures (IOPs).

A. Finding the Text of Federal Rules of Court

The *United States Code, United States Code Annotated*, and *United States Code Service* all include federal court rules. In the *United States Code*, the Federal Rules of Civil Procedure, Federal Rules of Appellate Procedure, Federal Rules of Evidence, and other rules are found in an appendix following the volume containing Title 28 on the Judiciary and Judicial Procedure. Similarly, the Federal Rules of Criminal Procedure are found in an appendix following Title 18 on Crimes and Criminal Procedure.

In the *United States Code Annotated* (U.S.C.A.), these rules also follow Title 18 and Title 28, but the rules are in special rules volumes. In the *United States Code Service* (U.S.C.S.), the rules are in special Courts Rules volumes at the end of the series. In both U.S.C.A. and U.S.C.S., be sure to check the pocket parts and supplemental paper volumes for current information.

West's deskbooks for each state include a companion volume containing rules for the federal courts located in that state. West's *Pennsylvania Rules of Court: Volume II—Federal* contains the Federal Rules of Civil Procedure, Federal Rules of Evidence, Federal Rules of Appellate Procedure, and Rules of Procedure of the Judicial Panel on MultiDistrict Litigation, among others.

West's *Federal Civil Judicial Procedure and Rules* includes the Federal Rules of Civil Procedure, Federal Rules of Evidence, Federal Rules of Appellate Procedure, and some federal statutes dealing with jurisdiction and procedure. Other deskbooks for federal rules also exist, such as *Moore's Federal Rules Pamphlet*, which is published in four volumes by Matthew Bender. Use the index or table of contents for these sources to find the rule or rules relevant to your issue.

Federal court rules are available online from a variety of sources. For example, federal court rules are available via the website for the Legal Information Institute (LII).[5] LII is a free research and publishing activity of the Cornell Law

---

5. LII's website is www.law.cornell.edu.

School. LLI provide links to federal court rules, including the Federal Rules of Evidence, Federal Rules of Bankruptcy Procedure, and Federal Rules of Civil Procedure.

The website for the federal judiciary provides access to the federal rules of practice and procedure in effect, information on the rulemaking process (including proposed rules and pending amendments), and archival records.[6] Available rules include the Federal Rules of Appellate Procedure, the Federal Rules of Bankruptcy Procedure, and the Federal Rules of Civil Procedure.

To find federal rules using Westlaw, Lexis Advance, or Bloomberg Law, use the databases dedicated to federal court rules. Westlaw has databases dedicated to specific federal rules, such as the Federal Rules of Appellate Procedure, the Federal Rules of Civil Procedure, the Federal Rules of Criminal Procedure, and the Federal Rules of Evidence. Browse the Westlaw directory for other specialized court rules databases. You can also conduct a search in the United States Code Annotated database. On Lexis Advance, search in the "U.S.C.S. — Federal Rules Annotated" database. Bloomberg Law also has multiple specialized databases, which may be accessed by clicking on the "Federal Law" tab from the main "Search and Browse" home page, and then clicking on "Federal Court Rules."

B. Finding the Text of Local Federal Rules of Court

Both U.S.C.A. and U.S.C.S. contain local rules of the federal circuits in volumes following the Federal Rules of Appellate Procedure. In both U.S.C.A. and U.S.C.S., be sure to check for pocket parts and supplemental paper volumes for current information.

West's *Pennsylvania Rules of Court: Volume II — Federal* contains the Third Circuit Local Appellate Rules and local rules for the federal district courts (including Bankruptcy Courts) sitting in Pennsylvania. Other information in the federal deskbook includes fee schedules for the various courts. Local rules are also available in *Federal Local Court Rules*, a looseleaf service published by West, which collects the local rules of each federal district court and each federal circuit court of appeals.

To find the text of local federal rules of court online, go to the website for The United States Courts[7] "Court Website Links." You will find links to

---

6. Check the "Rules and Policies" tab at www.uscourts.gov.
7. "Court Website Links" are available at www.uscourts.gov/about-federal-courts/federal-courts-public/court-website-links.

the websites for the United States Supreme Court, each of the United States Circuit Courts of Appeals, as well as all of the United States District Courts and Bankruptcy Courts. Local rules for each court are available on its individual website.

Local federal rules can also be accessed on Westlaw, Lexis Advance, and Bloomberg Law.

In Westlaw, local rules for each of the United States Courts of Appeals may be found in the U.S.C.A. database. Scroll down to the list of circuits, located between Titles 28 and 29. To find the rules of a federal district court or bankruptcy court, select "Statutes and Court Rules" from the "All Content" box on the Westlaw search home page. Next, click on the name of the state you want to research and browse the table of contents to find relevant local rules.

To find local rules for the United States Courts of Appeals on Lexis Advance, search or browse in the "U.S.C.S. Court Rules" database. To find local rules of court for a federal district court or bankruptcy court, select a state from the "Explore Content" box on the main research home page. Once you have selected a state, click on the link to that state's "Local, State & Federal Court Rules" database, which is located under the heading "Statutes and Legislation." Then enter your search terms.

On Bloomberg Law, local federal court rules may be accessed by clicking on the "Federal Law" tab from the main "Search and Browse" home page, and then clicking on one of the specialized local rules databases listed under "Federal Court Rules."

C. Interpreting Specific Rules of Court

As noted regarding Pennsylvania rules, you will need to do further research to determine how the rule should be interpreted and applied in your case. Most federal rules include advisory comments to help interpret the rules. These comments show what the drafters had in mind when they wrote the rule. These comments are not binding authority, but they are very persuasive.

One key way to interpret rules is to review case law that has applied the specific rule you have found. There are several ways to find citations to relevant cases. You may use U.S.C.A. and U.S.C.S. to find case annotations as well as advisory committee notes and research aids on each rule. You can also update the rule using KeyCite on Westlaw, or Shepard's on Lexis Advance.

Several services provide citations to cases interpreting rules. One such resource is *Federal Rules Service*, published by West, which indexes and reports decisions regarding the Federal Rules of Civil Procedure and the Federal Rules of Appellate Procedure. The *Federal Rules of Evidence Service*, also published by West, does the same for civil and criminal cases interpreting the Federal Rules of Evidence. The advantages of using this type of service are that they are often more current than any other print source, and some cases are not published anywhere else.

Treatises are additional sources for finding cases that interpret rules of court because the footnotes in treatises often contain references to cases on point. Treatises exist for each set of federal court rules. Search a library catalog or scan the stacks to find treatises on point. There are many well-respected treatises written on federal rules of procedure. Among the most widely recognized are Wright & Miller's *Federal Practice and Procedure*, published by West and also available on Westlaw, and *Moore's Federal Practice*, published by LexisNexis and available on Lexis Advance. While these are based on treatises written years ago, they are kept current by professors and practitioners. Some other helpful treatises include *Bender's Federal Practice Manual* and *Weinstein's Federal Evidence*, published by LexisNexis and also available on Lexis Advance.

Cases that interpret federal rules are published in the West reporter called *Federal Rules Decisions* (F.R.D.). F.R.D. reports federal court decisions issued by United States District Courts regarding the Federal Rules of Civil Procedure and the Federal Rules of Criminal Procedure. Opinions appearing in F.R.D. have not been designated for publication in the *Federal Supplement*. Cases interpreting court rules are also available on Westlaw, Lexis Advance, and Bloomberg Law.

IV. Rules of Ethics

A. Pennsylvania Rules of Ethics

Pennsylvania professional ethics for lawyers are governed by the Pennsylvania Rules of Professional Conduct. The Pennsylvania Rules of Professional Conduct are based on the Model Rules of Professional Conduct, drafted by the American Bar Association, which are the basis for rules regulating lawyers in every state. Pennsylvania judges are also governed by the Code of Judicial Conduct. The Rules of Professional Conduct and Code of Judicial Conduct set high standards for the practice of law and the conduct of judges. For example, Canon 1 of the Code of Judicial Conduct requires judges to "uphold and promote the independence, integrity, and impartiality of the judiciary," and to "avoid impropriety and the appearance of impropriety."

The Preamble to the Rules of Professional Conduct notes the lawyer's three concurrent roles as representative of clients, officer of the legal system, and public citizen with special responsibilities for the quality of justice. The rules then delineate requirements and prohibitions for a lawyer's conduct in fulfilling these obligations. For example, the rules require that lawyers work to expedite litigation[8] and prohibit filing frivolous claims.[9] The rules cover relationships with clients, other parties, opposing counsel, witnesses, and the court. Of special importance as a lawyer prepares documents for a court is Rule 3.3, which imposes on each lawyer a duty to truthfully disclose all material facts and law. This rule specifically requires a lawyer to disclose controlling legal authority that is adverse to the lawyer's client and not disclosed by the opposing side.[10]

Official comments further explain the rules. For example, Rule 5.2 states that a lawyer working as a subordinate for another lawyer is bound by the professional conduct rules, but does not violate the rules by complying with a supervisory lawyer's reasonable request. The comment to that rule explains that the subordinate lawyer is not relieved of responsibility because she acted at the direction of a supervisor. Instead, the fact that she was acting pursuant to a supervisor's directions would be a relevant fact in determining whether the subordinate attorney had the knowledge required to render her conduct a violation of the Pennsylvania Rules of Professional Conduct.

Pennsylvania ethical rules are annotated in Title 42 of *Purdon's Pennsylvania Statutes and Consolidated Statutes Annotated*, which contain judicial constructions and historical notes. They are also included in the West deskbook, *Pennsylvania Rules of Court: Volume I — State*.

Free access to the text of Pennsylvania ethical rules is available online. The Pennsylvania Rules of Professional Conduct are available on the website for the Pennsylvania Code[11] under Title 204 — Judicial System General Provisions, Part V — Professional Ethics and Conduct. The Pennsylvania Rules of Professional Conduct are also accessible from the website for the Disciplinary Board of the Supreme Court of Pennsylvania,[12] under the "Attorneys" tab. The text of Pennsylvania ethical rules is also available on Westlaw, Lexis Advance and Bloomberg Law. The easiest way to find the text of a rule is to type the citation directly into the search box on the home page of any of these platforms.

The Pennsylvania Code of Judicial Conduct is available on the website for the Judicial Conduct Board of Pennsylvania.[13] The Judicial Conduct Board of

---

8. Pa. R. Prof. Conduct 3.2.
9. Pa. R. Prof. Conduct 3.1.
10. Pa. R. Prof. Conduct 3.3(a)(2).
11. www.pacode.com.
12. www.padisciplinaryboard.org.
13. http://judicialconductboardofpa.org.

Pennsylvania is a twelve-member panel of Pennsylvania citizens, who are charged with investigating allegations of misconduct against Pennsylvania judges. When necessary, the Judicial Conduct Board of Pennsylvania prepares and brings cases against attorneys who are accused of unethical actions. The Pennsylvania Code of Judicial Conduct and other ethical rules applying to the Pennsylvania judiciary may also be accessed online at the website for the Pennsylvania Code under Chapter 207—Judicial Conduct. In additional, formal opinions interpreting the Pennsylvania Code of Judicial Conduct, which are issued by the Ethics Committee of the Pennsylvania Conference of State Trial Judges, are also available on the Pennsylvania Code website.

To find cases interpreting the rules, use the annotated statutes, either in print or online. You can also use a digest or the key number system to locate cases that interpret the rules. In *West's Pennsylvania Digest 2d*, for example, topics relating to legal ethics are listed under the heading "Attorneys and Clients." You can also find cases interpreting the rules on Westlaw, Lexis Advance, and Bloomberg Law by conducting a keyword search and adding an ethical rule as a search term. In addition, ethics opinions issued by the Pennsylvania Bar Association, Legal Ethics and Professional Responsibility Committee are available to members of the Pennsylvania Bar on the bar association website.[14]

Because Pennsylvania rules are patterned after ABA model rules, ABA resources can be helpful in researching ethical issues. The ABA issues formal opinions on ethics subjects. These opinions are merely persuasive; they are not binding authority. The ABA publishes these opinions in *Formal Ethics Opinions*. They are also available via the online subscription service, *ABA/BNA Lawyers' Manual on Professional Conduct*, which is published by Bloomberg BNA. ABA ethics opinions can also be accessed online via the website for the ABA Center for Professional Responsibility.[15] However, the full archive of formal ethics opinions is only available to members of the ABA Center for Professional Responsibility. The model rules, with commentary, are available in a series published by the ABA Center for Professional Responsibility called *Annotated Model Rules of Professional Conduct*. The *Pennsylvania Ethics Handbook* published by PBI Press is a useful resource because it incorporates the amendments to the Pennsylvania Rules of Professional Conduct drawn from the ABA Ethics 20/20 Commission Report. Treatises on legal ethics, such as the American Law Institute's *Restatement of the Law Third, The Law Governing Lawyers*, available from West, can also be helpful.

---

14. www.pabar.org/public/committees/lglethic.
15. www.americanbar.org/groups/professional_responsibility.html.

B. Federal Rules of Ethics

No uniform set of ethical rules governs the practice of law in the federal courts. Instead, Pennsylvania attorneys practicing in federal courts are expected to abide by the ethical rules set forth within the local rules governing each court. For example, Local Appellate Rules for the Third Circuit set forth sanctions for attorney misconduct under L.A.R. Misc. 107 through 107.4. Potential sanctions for failing to comply with the Federal Rules of Appellate Procedure include dismissal of an appeal, striking of the non-complying document, imposition of costs, or disciplinary sanctions upon counsel.

The district courts also set forth ethical rules within each court's local rules of civil procedure. For example, in the Eastern District of Pennsylvania, Local Rule of Civil Procedure 83.6 governs attorney conduct when handling civil cases. The rules govern ethical subjects, such as attorneys convicted of crimes, disbarment, discipline, and standards for professional conduct.

The Code of Conduct for United States Judges is a set of ethical canons adopted by the Judicial Conference of the United States. The Code of Conduct for United States Judges is available online on the website for the United States Courts under the "Judges and Judgeships" tab. The Code of Conduct applies to United States circuit court judges, district court judges, and the judges of several specialized courts. For example, Canon 2 provides that "[a] judge should avoid impropriety and the appearance of impropriety." Furthermore, Canon 2(A) provides that "[a] judge should not hold membership in any organization that practices invidious discrimination on the basis of race, sex, religion, or national origin." Commentary is included for some of the canons, along with a few citations to primary authority.

The Judicial Conference of the United States has also authorized its Committee on Codes of Conduct to publish formal advisory opinions. The purpose of the advisory opinions is to provide ethical guidance for judges and judicial employees on issues that are frequently raised or have broad application. Published advisory opinions may be accessed at www.uscourts.gov, under the "Rules and Policies" tab. Additional Judicial Conference Regulations governing gifts and outside earned income, honoraria, and employment may also be accessed under the "Rules and Policies" tab.

Chapter 8

Secondary Sources

As explained in Chapter 1, *secondary sources* are sources that discuss, describe, or comment on the law without having the force of law themselves. Examples of secondary sources include law review articles, legal encyclopedias, and treatises.

Secondary sources can help you find shortcuts to primary authority and can give you the background or context you need to understand an issue or an area of the law. You must remember, however, that only primary authorities have the force of law. When you are analyzing a problem, predicting how a court will rule, or trying to convince a court to agree with your position, your goal will be to locate whatever primary authority is available.

The opening section of this chapter covers general principles about using secondary sources. The chapter then addresses more specific information about several types of general legal secondary sources. The first sources described are treatises, legal encyclopedias, and *American Law Reports* (ALR) articles covering specific legal topics. The chapter concludes with two sources that tend to be more scholarly: legal periodicals and Restatements of the Law.

I. Secondary Sources in General

A. When to Use Secondary Sources

As a rule, unless the goal of your research is extremely limited, begin with a secondary source when researching an unfamiliar area of law. Taking the time to do this background reading will help you develop a research vocabulary and will help you put the primary sources you read into context.

It is less crucial to begin research with a secondary source if you are familiar enough with an area of law to know where you are most likely to find relevant primary authorities. Secondary sources can be a shortcut to primary authorities, so it is often helpful to consult them even when you have some background knowledge already. As your research progresses, you will often find that reading secondary sources helps clarify your own analysis of a problem.

As you become more of an expert in certain areas, you will rely on secondary sources less for basic explanations or overviews and more as sources of commentary, policy, and current developments in the law. This does not mean you will stop using them in your research. Even experienced attorneys are regularly confronted with problems they have not had to solve before and can benefit from what a wide range of secondary sources have to offer.

B. Choosing Secondary Sources

An enormous amount of legal commentary, background sources, and practice-oriented materials is available to you. With experience, you will learn to prefer certain sources for certain types of issues. The descriptions below include information about when each type of secondary source will most likely be helpful. You will develop your own preferences with experience.

If you are beginning research in an area of law with which you are unfamiliar, you might find broad and general secondary sources, such as treatises and legal encyclopedias, the most helpful. In some states, a state-specific legal encyclopedia often will serve as a shortcut to understanding basic rules of law and direct you to primary sources that illustrate the rules in that jurisdiction. For example, *Pennsylvania Law Encyclopedia 2d* and *Summary of Pennsylvania Jurisprudence 2d* summarize Pennsylvania law. More general legal encyclopedias also can be used to find primary sources, but they are not always helpful in researching the law of a specific state. Once you have narrowed your issue or if you are researching an issue with which you are familiar, you might choose sources that analyze more narrow points of law, such as *ALR* articles or law review articles.

Do not feel you have to keep searching for every conceivable secondary source that might address your issue. Once you have developed a research vocabulary and have identified the issues your research must address, continue your research using primary sources. You can always return to secondary sources to help clarify your analysis.[1]

C. Whether to Use Print or Online Secondary Sources

Some researchers prefer using secondary sources in print. The printed page may feel more readable and have fewer visual distractions than an online ver-

---

1. Keep good notes about the sources you have consulted and photocopy or print only specific portions that you will refer to as you write.

sion, and a print layout and font may be more conducive to reading. Conversely, many researchers prefer using online secondary sources because they are full-text searchable, hyperlink to related primary and secondary sources, are more accessible, and may speed up the research process. Some online secondary sources include PDFs of the print version, thus, providing the advantages associated with using both print and online formats.

In addition to one's personal preference, a consideration in looking for secondary sources is that their availability sometimes changes if the publisher changes or if the publisher reaches a new agreement with West or Lexis. If a state encyclopedia formerly published by a Lexis affiliate is taken over by a West affiliate, you may only be able to access the online version if you are a Westlaw subscriber. The print version of the encyclopedia will still be on the same shelf.

Practically speaking, access provided to general secondary sources through West and Lexis is fairly comparable despite the differing titles. For example, although West publishes *Summary of Pennsylvania Jurisprudence 2d*, Lexis publishes *Pennsylvania Law Encyclopedia 2d*. Both are legal encyclopedias covering a broad range of specific Pennsylvania topics.

Whether to use print or online secondary sources most likely will be determined by what is available to you—for example, a print treatise, online access to *Summary of Pennsylvania Jurisprudence 2d* through Westlaw, or online access to *American Law Reports* through Lexis Advance. Even if you do not have access to secondary sources in print or through Westlaw or Lexis Advance, you can still access some secondary sources online through open access resources, which will be discussed later in this chapter.

D. Updating and Citing Secondary Sources

Some secondary sources can be Shepardized or KeyCited to see whether they have been cited in court opinions. This can be a clue to whether a certain source is well respected, but Shepardizing or KeyCiting will not tell you whether a secondary source still reflects the most current information available.

As you start to use various sources, you will see that there are other methods for determining whether your source reflects the current state of the law. Checking the scope notes of online secondary sources may be helpful in determining currency, but scope notes are only as useful as the depth of your understanding of the specific secondary source and how frequently, if at all, the source is updated. Many print sources include pocket parts or paper supplements, which should be checked diligently. Even though secondary sources cannot be overruled, it is important to update your research.

When drafting a memo or legal document, remember that the text of a secondary source is never binding authority. Even an article or treatise written by a renowned expert is, at best, persuasive. When citing secondary sources, you will often need to use signals and parenthetical phrases to explain to the reader how the source is helpful.

II. Treatises

A. Overview

A legal treatise is simply a book that extensively covers an area of law. Treatises are invaluable as introductions to a subject area and can be helpful in locating primary sources. Treatises may include exhaustive surveys of the law of a given area, scholarly discussions of an area, analyses of new legal developments, or concise explanations of a legal topic geared towards students.

B. Locating and Using Treatises

One route to finding treatises is to search your library's online catalog by keyword, title, or subject. Many library catalogs now include records to both print and online versions of treatises available through that library. For online treatises, you can click directly from the catalog record to the online treatise. For print treatises, the catalog records contain call numbers, which are assigned based on subject matter. For example, if the book *Property* by Joseph Singer is assigned the call number KF570 S56 2017, that call number translates as follows: K means it is about law, KF means it is about U.S. law, 570 means it is about property, S56 indicates the author's last name, and 2017 is the year it was published. Once you know the call number of a pertinent book, you can use that number to locate the book on the shelf or ask a librarian to help you. Then browse the nearby shelves for other relevant books that title or keyword searching alone may not have revealed.

If you are using Westlaw or Lexis Advance, look in the general content category *Secondary Sources* (Westlaw) or *Secondary Materials* (Lexis Advance) for *Treatises*. Once in the specific *Treatises* category, you can keyword search all treatises or filter by legal topic or jurisdiction. Bloomberg Law provides a limited number of treatises on specialized topics, which can be located in the category *Books & Treatises*.

Many law library websites provide legal research guides on various topics, which include suggestions for relevant treatises. Simply use a search engine, such as Google, to keyword search your legal topic and the phrase "research guide." For example, Googling "criminal law research guide" might direct you to Georgetown Law Library's Criminal Law and Justice Research Guide, which contains suggested treatises discussing that topic. Typically, these research guides link directly to the treatises available on Westlaw, Lexis Advance, and Bloomberg Law. For print titles, research guides link to the catalog records of that specific library. To find out if your library has that treatise, simply use the title from the research guide to search your library's catalog.

Georgetown Law Library and Yale Law Library provide free online *treatise finders*. In addition to suggesting treatises for dozens of legal topics, the authoring librarians identify which of the titles are considered preeminent treatises (or study aids) and their availability online. As with research guides, treatise finders link directly to the treatises available on Westlaw, Lexis Advance, and Bloomberg Law and to the catalog records of that specific library for print titles. Again, simply use the title from the treatise finder to search your library's catalog to see if your library has that treatise.

Another way to find a treatise is to check the casebooks and hornbooks you already have.[2] Many casebooks and hornbooks contain a list of legal texts from the same publisher, and they frequently cross-reference sister publications. Checking which treatises these publications cite in discussions about your particular topic can be a useful tool.

Once you have located a relevant treatise, use the table of contents and index to pinpoint discussions of specific topics. In print, the table of contents typically is located at the beginning of the treatise and outlines the content covered from the first to last page, while the index typically is located at the end of the treatise and provides an alphabetical listing of topics by keyword along with the corresponding page numbers on which the topics are discussed. On Westlaw, the table of contents is presented once you click on the treatise title, and the index is located in the Tools & Resources box to the right of the table of contents. On Lexis Advance, the table of contents can be viewed by

---

2. A casebook is not a treatise. It collects fragments of cases and other authorities with only limited commentary or explanation of the authorities. Casebooks are rarely consulted outside of the legal classroom. A hornbook is, in contrast, a very basic treatise that can be helpful in refreshing your memory about basic legal concepts, particularly in fundamental subjects like torts, contracts, and civil procedure. Hornbooks are less useful as a springboard to primary authorities than many other treatises and secondary sources, but they and other basic treatises, such as the *Nutshell* and *Understanding* series, should not be overlooked as starting points for understanding an unfamiliar area of law. They generally have only limited case citations but make up for that with concise explanations of the basic concepts you will be analyzing.

clicking on the table of contents icon to the right of the treatise title, and the index is included at the beginning of the table of contents.

C. The Role of Treatises in Your Research

Treatises are often an excellent place to begin research, especially in an unfamiliar area. They can also be helpful starting points when you are researching areas of the law that are well established. By starting with a treatise instead of going directly to cases or annotated statutes, you can save considerable time and frustration. Even if the treatise does not cite a relevant case or statute in your jurisdiction, it will help you develop a list of keywords to use in searching those primary authorities.

Some treatises attempt to summarize a body of law in a single volume. These are most helpful for learning basic rules of law and avoiding outdated or discredited ones. Other treatises are multi-volume works containing extensive case citations to a number of jurisdictions. A third type of treatise is written with practitioners in mind. These treatises are written by practitioners and explain specific aspects of state law. They often include commentary on specific issues, advice about procedural considerations, what to consider when drafting forms, and sample forms. For example, if you need information on how to pursue a certain type of legal claim in Pennsylvania, you might consult *Standard Pennsylvania Practice 2d*, an established treatise on the mechanics of civil and criminal procedure in the Commonwealth. Do not assume that a treatise will not be helpful just because your problem is specific; treatises exist on an endless variety of topics.

If you need information about the law of several or all states, you will find treatises devoted to surveys of the law. These treatises provide an in-depth analysis of each state's laws regarding a specific area. For example, there are state-by-state treatises devoted to trade secrets, covenants not to compete, and wage and hour laws, among other legal issues.

D. Updating Treatises

Some single-volume books are only updated by the publication of subsequent editions. Consequently, even an authoritative work may be less helpful in research than a more recent publication by a different author. Many treatises are updated, however, meaning that they are revised or supplemented to reflect changes in the law. Print multi-volume treatises are often published in looseleaf binders that allow discussions of new cases to be added without reprinting the entire volume. Sometimes discussions of new cases are simply inserted at the beginning of the volume with cross-references to the sections in the main part of the volume. Other print treatises are supplemented using pocket parts or paperbound supplements. For online treatises, updates are typically incorporated into the text instead of appending the treatise with separate supplements. Whether you are using print or online treatises, always check the publication date of the treatise and if it has been subsequently updated.

III. Legal Encyclopedias

A. Overview

Legal encyclopedias cover an extensive range of topics. In contrast to treatises, which provide an in-depth analysis of one legal topic, legal encyclopedias provide a general overview of a broad range of legal topics. Although the overviews are general, they are usually supported by extensive footnotes to cases from state and federal jurisdictions that illustrate the point of law being discussed. Typically, legal encyclopedias are arranged alphabetically by topic.

In Pennsylvania, two separate encyclopedias summarize state law: *Summary of Pennsylvania Jurisprudence 2d* (West) and *Pennsylvania Law Encyclopedia 2d* (Lexis). Because different publishers publish them, they are organized differently and contain different cross-references. State encyclopedias can be helpful, especially when discussing established areas of the law, and will direct you to a variety of primary sources and practice aids.

Two national law encyclopedias contain entries on the law of all American jurisdictions. They are *Corpus Juris Secundum* (C.J.S.), which is available on Westlaw, and *American Jurisprudence 2d* (Am. Jur. 2d),[3] which is available on both Westlaw and Lexis Advance. Due to the wide scope of their coverage, national encyclopedias will not always lead you to cases from the jurisdiction you are working in. Although they do not focus on the law of specific jurisdictions, they usually indicate when there is a split of authority on a point of law.

B. Locating and Using Encyclopedias

Choosing an encyclopedia sometimes depends on whether your issue is limited to a single jurisdiction or potentially requires finding authority from mul-

---

3. Some legal research texts discuss cross-referencing between older and newer versions of both encyclopedias. This is not typically a problem unless you are researching a relatively obscure issue or preparing a manuscript that requires exhaustive historical research into a certain topic. If this is the case, a reference librarian should be able to help you with the necessary cross-referencing.

tiple jurisdictions. In any jurisdiction where a state law encyclopedia is available, that encyclopedia will be more likely to lead to relevant primary authorities than one of the national encyclopedias. Choosing between the two national encyclopedias is largely a matter of personal preference. Some people find one more helpful than another; others like the quantity of footnotes in one or the cross-references in another.[4]

One consideration to keep in mind when using encyclopedias is that encyclopedias published by one of the major legal publishers tend to cross-reference other sources from the same publisher. This means, for example, that C.J.S. and other West encyclopedias, like the *Summary of Pennsylvania Jurisprudence 2d*, will have cross-references to the West key number system and to other sources published by West. This can be a helpful shortcut to finding cases.

Regardless of the publisher, encyclopedias typically have several different finding tools allowing you to locate information within the series. They are arranged in broad subject areas, which are called titles or topics. Each title or topic is further subdivided into sections and subsections. Typically, a title or topic begins with both a general and a detailed outline of its contents. If you already know (from experience or from some other source) what title or topic you need to consult, you can go directly to one of these outlines to find pertinent sections and subsections. In Am. Jur. 2d, the beginning of each general topic contains "Treated Elsewhere" cross-references, which can be helpful in locating more specific treatments of certain issues.

If you do not already know the title or topic you need to consult, encyclopedias also typically have detailed and helpful indices. In print, they are usually in separate volumes, which may be paperback volumes to allow for updating. The indices will refer you to a title or topic, as well as to a section number, that corresponds to the keyword(s) you are searching for. The print version of Am. Jur. 2d also provides tables, such as a table of federal statutes discussed in various places in the encyclopedia to help you find pertinent sections.

If you are using Westlaw or Lexis Advance, look in the general content category *Secondary Sources* (Westlaw) or *Secondary Materials* (Lexis Advance). Legal encyclopedias are located in the specific category *Texts & Treatises* on Westlaw and *Jurisprudence* on Lexis Advance. Once in the specific category for

---

4. The original goal of the C.J.S. publishers was to include every reported case in American law. This is no longer true; however, some sections in C.J.S. will still have a greater number of footnoted references than comparable sections in Am. Jur. 2d. On the other hand, Am. Jur. 2d sections will often include references to A.L.R. annotations, discussed below, and to other secondary sources that do not appear in C.J.S.

encyclopedias, you can keyword search all encyclopedias or filter by jurisdiction, which is an effective way to ascertain if a state-specific encyclopedia is available. Within a specific encyclopedia—C.J.S., Am. Jur. 2d, *Summary of Pennsylvania Jurisprudence*, etc.—you can full-text keyword search, use the index, or use the table of contents.

C. The Role of Encyclopedias in Your Research

Like some basic treatises, encyclopedias provide a broad overview of the law. They are most useful early in your research. A state law encyclopedia may be more helpful on issues within a particular jurisdiction than national encyclopedias, but even a state law encyclopedia is most helpful as a starting point rather than as an aid to understanding an especially complicated or novel issue. Keep in mind that there can be a long lead time between developments in the law and their addition to an encyclopedia; they are rarely a good source of recent developments.

D. Updating Encyclopedias

Print encyclopedia volumes are typically supplemented with pocket parts and, when the pocket part becomes too large, paperback supplements. The pocket parts and supplements can contain additional text as well as recent citations to other sources, so these updating tools should always be consulted, even when you are just reading the source for general background information. From time to time, an entire volume will be reprinted. Print Am. Jur. 2d also has a New Topic Service contained in a separate binder that is shelved with the Am. Jur. 2d index volumes. While pocket parts supplement topics that already appear in the bound volumes, the New Topic Service contains entirely new topics, along with citations to cases and annotations. For online encyclopedias, updates are typically incorporated into the text instead of appending the encyclopedias with pocket parts and supplements.

IV. *American Law Reports*

A. Overview

American Law Reports, or A.L.R., is source of commentary about a wide variety of specific legal issues. The original goal of A.L.R. was to serve as a highly selective case reporter; over time it has come to be used primarily for its detailed annotations, now called articles. Article topics are often similar to periodical articles in scope and length. They address narrow topics in detail rather than providing broad overviews of an area of law, and they provide a multijurisdictional survey of case law on the specific topic covered.

For example, a legal encyclopedia might have a general overview of a landowner's duties to those who enter her land. An A.L.R. article, on the other hand, might address the landowner's duty to a specific category of persons (social guests, rescue personnel, undiscovered trespassers) and would identify conflicts in the law or splits in authority on that particular point.[5]

A.L.R. has been published in several series. The series you are most likely to use are those published within the last fifty years: A.L.R.3d, A.L.R.4th, A.L.R.5th, A.L.R.6th, A.L.R.7th, and three sets of federal law annotations, A.L.R. Fed., A.L.R. Fed. 2d, and A.L.R. Fed. 3d. The non-federal series deal almost exclusively with state law topics (volumes of A.L.R.3d published between 1965 and 1969 contain federal law topics as well); the three federal series deal specifically with federal law from 1969 to the present.

B. Locating and Using A.L.R. Articles

Unlike a legal encyclopedia, A.L.R. is not organized according to topic. You cannot expect to find a related topic in the main volume and flip through to find your topic discussed nearby. Thus, developing a good research vocabulary is essential to finding an A.L.R. article on point.

Both the print and online versions of A.L.R. have indices. Use the A.L.R. Index just as you use other indices: search for keywords and topics, which will lead you to relevant articles.

In print, A.L.R.2d through A.L.R.7th and the federal series are currently indexed together. The federal series has its own Quick Index, but that index refers you only to federal articles, not to the other series. Unless you are sure you can limit your research to federal law, you should use the broader index to be sure you do not miss pertinent annotations. If you are researching a specific statute, rule, or regulation, you can start with the Table of Laws, Rules,

---

5. As an example, the following titles come from 1 A.L.R.6th: "Validity and Applicability of Statutory Time Limit Concerning Taxpayer's Claim for State Tax Refund"; "Validity of Warrantless Search of Motor Vehicle Passenger Based on Odor of Marijuana"; "Effect of Appointment of Legal Representative for Minor on Running of State Statute of Limitations Against Minor"; and "Right to Credit on Child Support for Health Insurance, Medical, Dental, and Orthodontic Expenses Paid for Child's Benefit While Child Is Not Living with Obligor Parent."

and Regulations in the back of the print index. The table will lead you directly to annotations citing your primary source.

If you are using Westlaw or Lexis Advance, look in the general content category *Secondary Sources* (Westlaw) or *Secondary Materials* (Lexis Advance). A.L.R. is its own specific category *American Law Reports* on Westlaw, but it is included under the category *Jurisprudence* on Lexis Advance. Once in A.L.R., you can full-text keyword search the entire A.L.R. series, filter by topic, or use the comprehensive online index.

Each article begins with a description of the scope and a table of contents. The Article Outline, Index, and a Table of Cases, Laws, and Rules allow you to click directly to article commentary and primary authority pertinent to your research. You should skim the Research References before reading the entire article because you may find that another article addresses your issue more directly.

C. The Role of A.L.R. in Your Research

Because A.L.R. articles are specific reports on limited legal issues rather than general overviews of an area of law, you may want to turn to A.L.R. only when you are familiar with the general area of law you are researching. If you know enough about your topic to frame it somewhat narrowly, you may choose to start your research with an A.L.R. article.

Once you have determined that an article is on point, you can review it to find citations to primary authority on your issue. You can also use it to find extensive cross-references to other A.L.R. articles, encyclopedia entries, practice tools, and cases (using West key numbers). In addition to the sources listed in the article, the case accompanying the article can lead to more cases through the use of key numbers and citators.

D. Updating A.L.R. Articles

In print, pocket parts are used to supplement bound A.L.R. volumes, including index and digest volumes. An entire article will sometimes be superseded by a new article to reflect changes in the law. Always check to see whether an article is still current before you read and rely on it. The pocket parts indicate whether an entire annotation has been superseded, as opposed to supplemented. Also, the print A.L.R. Index contains a comprehensive Annotation History Table.

Online A.L.R. articles are kept current with the weekly addition of new cases, and cumulative supplemental information is incorporated into the relevant sections of the article. If an article has been superseded by a new article, it is noted and a hyperlink to the new article is provided. A.L.R. articles can be KeyCited or Shepardized to see if they have been cited in other legal sources.

V. Legal Periodicals

A. Overview

Legal periodicals publish articles on every aspect of the law, with emphasis ranging from the extremely theoretical to solidly practical. Many legal periodicals are published in the form of law reviews. Law review articles are often a good place to start learning about an unfamiliar area because they summarize the law, analyze new developments in the law, and provide background information on important cases and new statutes. Law reviews are generally published by students at law schools, although some are exclusively written and edited by experts in a given field. Each law school has a law review or journal that publishes articles on a variety of topics. Most law schools also have specialized journals devoted to such areas as environmental law, civil rights, or tax. Law schools within a particular state often devote specific issues to recent legislation or case law developments from that jurisdiction. Law reviews or journals are usually published in more than one volume throughout the year.

Law reviews contain several different types of articles. Those specifically labeled Articles are generally written by practitioners or scholars, not students, and provide in-depth analysis of a specific, sometimes narrow point of law. Occasionally, they will contain a survey of a particular area instead of analysis of a narrow topic. A typical student-written piece is a Case Comment, which analyzes a single case in depth. Students also write Notes, which analyze a specific area of law and may be as long and detailed as articles.

Legal periodicals also encompass bar journals, bar newspapers, and journals specific to a certain topic area or type of practice. These publications tend to be more practical than scholarly, and are discussed in Chapter 9, Practice Materials. Because they tend to have shorter publication schedules than scholarly journals, they can be good sources of information on recent developments or in areas of the law that are evolving in your jurisdiction.

When selecting an article to read, relying on an article in formulating or deepening your analysis, or deciding whether to cite an article in your written work, you must take into account the persuasive value of the article. There are no hard-and-fast rules for preferring one source to another. In general, you will prefer an article written by an expert or practitioner in a field to one written by a student. However, there is no reason to totally disregard student pieces. Given the amount of research necessary to prepare a piece for publication, a law student may know more about a particular topic than many practitioners. Student pieces can be particularly helpful in summarizing or surveying the developments in a field. Regardless of authorship, the footnotes in most articles have been gathered and verified by student editors. Tips for choosing articles are summarized in Table 8-1.

Table 8-1. How to Choose an Article

Acceptance:	Has the article already been widely cited as authoritative by courts or other writers?
Date:	How recent is the article? In rapidly changing areas of law, you will usually want to start with the most recent articles you can find. In an area that is relatively stable or when you are researching the evolution of a law or doctrine, you may find useful information in an older article.
Author:	Is the author already recognized as an authority in the field? If the biographical information about the author reveals that the author is a practitioner, scholar, or judge, it is relatively easy to find out what some of the author's other publications are and to get an idea of how frequently the author has published in the past.
Journal:	Is the journal published in your jurisdiction? Is it widely respected?
Depth:	Is the article solidly supported with reference to both primary and secondary authorities?
Use:	How do you plan to use the article? If you plan to cite to it as persuasive authority, the preceding factors become increasingly important. If you plan to simply mine the article's citations and footnotes for research, those factors become less important.

B. Locating and Using Periodicals

The *Index to Legal Periodicals* (ILP), *Legal Source,* and the *Legal Resource Index* (LRI) are three popular, online indexing products for law review articles. Most academic law libraries provide online access to ILP or *Legal Source* from their website or catalog, and the LRI can be accessed through Westlaw. Your library may also have access to the *Current Index to Legal Periodicals* (CILP), which publishes new articles by topic or subject on a weekly basis, and the *Index to Foreign Legal Periodicals,* which is helpful in researching issues of international law.

If you are using Westlaw or Lexis Advance, look in the general content category *Secondary Sources* (Westlaw) or *Secondary Materials* (Lexis Advance). Legal periodicals are located in the specific category *Law Reviews & Journals*. After you select that specific category, you can keyword search all journals or filter by legal topic or jurisdiction. Once in a specific title, you can full-text keyword search or search specific fields.

There are several other subscription-based services used for locating articles in legal periodicals. Two of the more popular ones are JSTOR and HeinOnline.

JSTOR is an online archive of scholarly articles containing a wide range of academic disciplines, including law, which are full-text searchable. JSTOR does not contain the full text of very recent articles, and its coverage varies depending on its agreement with specific publishers. If your research requires consulting extra-legal commentary sources or law review articles that may not be available through Westlaw or Lexis Advance, JSTOR can be an extremely valuable tool. Most academic libraries subscribe to JSTOR.

Many academic libraries also subscribe to an online service called HeinOnline, which provides journal articles online in PDF format, so that what you see on the screen is what you would have read in the print journal. Like JSTOR, HeinOnline does not have the text of many recent journals (which are often available on the website of the journal or law school in question), but it makes up for that with an archive that, in many cases, goes back to the original volume of the publication. For example, as of the spring of 2017, HeinOnline contained copies of *Temple Law Review* from 1927 through 2015, *University of Pennsylvania Law Review* from 1852 through 2015, and *University of Pittsburgh Law Review* from 1935 to 2015.[6]

Although Westlaw, Lexis Advance, JSTOR, and HeinOnline are paid subscription services, several open access options exist for locating journal articles online. These options include bepress Digital Commons Network, Social Science Research Network (SSRN), and law journal websites.

Over the last few years, implementation of institutional repositories has increased among academic institutions, particularly law schools. Schools use institutional repositories to make faculty scholarship more discoverable and accessible on the web. One of the most popular institutional repository products used is hosted by a company called bepress. Articles published through individual institutional repositories using the bepress product are also indexed in

---

6. In addition to legal periodicals, HeinOnline provides online access to United States treaties and international agreements, Supreme Court opinions, Attorney General Opinions, federal legislative histories, historical state session laws, and much more.

the bepress Digital Commons Network, which is searchable and open access. Most articles can be downloaded freely from the Network.[7]

Like bepress Digital Commons, SSRN is an online repository of scholarly works. Unlike Digital Commons, though, SSRN does not provide institutional level repositories schools can publish on their own websites. Among academics and researchers, it is a popular service for making scholarship more discoverable and accessible. You can freely search and download articles authors have added to SSRN.

A number of open access legal journals are available online now as well. You can search the content of current journal issues, as well as archived issues. Accessibility to archived issues varies from journal to journal. Examples of open access journals available online include *Duke Law Journal, Michigan Law Review, Texas Law Review,* and *Villanova Law Review.*

Another very useful online resource for finding articles is Google Scholar, which is a customized Google search for scholarly articles and book chapters from a broad range of disciplines. Instead of searching the open web as would be done with a general Google search, Google Scholar searches a subset of websites and subscription databases containing scholarly content, including Google Books; ProQuest; EBSCO; HeinOnline; JSTOR; Lexis; online repositories, such as SSRN and bepress Digital Commons Network; and university websites. Although Google Scholar uses full-text searching with results based on a proprietary algorithm, in some respects it acts as an indexing service across both subscription and open access services. This can be a useful resource for searching across many online services at once, especially if you have access to a library that subscribes to some of these services, which most academic libraries do. In addition to retrieving basic information about articles, you can click directly from the Google Scholar results into these services to retrieve articles if you are on a recognized library network. Despite only searching a subset of the web, the results from Google Scholar are still often too voluminous and irrelevant, but it can be a helpful resource when you do not have access to an indexing service.

C. The Role of Periodical Articles in Your Research

Law review articles are often a good place to begin your research because they are extensively footnoted with citations to primary authority. Footnotes to primary authority are helpful whether the author of an article is a student or a scholar. Also, law review articles will often give surveys or overviews of

---

7. As of spring 2017 law was the most represented discipline in the Network, constituting over 315,000 works and 93,000,000 downloads.

the law that will be helpful to introduce you to a topic. Some articles may be so specialized that, without a general knowledge of the subject area, you will not be able to put the article in context.

Law review articles also can be helpful in analyzing changing or controversial areas, because many authors write articles to critique existing or proposed laws. Remember that a single author's position does not necessarily reflect the state of the law or scholarly opinion. Do your own analysis of the pertinent cases or statutes.

Do not feel you must read a given number of articles before proceeding to the next step in your research. Keep the goal of your research in mind. Most of the time, that goal will be understanding the area of law at issue and locating primary authority.

D. Updating Periodical Articles

Unlike most other legal research materials, law review articles and other periodicals are never updated. Once an article is published, it is not revised and brought up-to-date with subsequent developments in the law. You cannot be sure an article still correctly describes the state of the law without doing further research. You can find out whether courts or other writers have cited a scholarly article by using KeyCite or Shepard's, but to find out whether the article represents the current state of the law, you will need to update the primary sources on which it relies.

VI. *Restatements of the Law*

A. Overview

Restatements of the Law (Restatements) are scholarly treatments of areas of the law that attempt to set forth black letter rules of common law.[8] For issues governed by common law, Restatements are among the most persuasive and most often cited of secondary sources. If your research issue is governed exclusively by statutory or administrative law, however, the Restatements will not help you find primary authority on point.

---

8. While Restatements of the Law are addressed to courts, Principles of the Law are addressed to legislatures and agencies (https://www.ali.org/publications/frequently-asked-questions/#differ).

If your issue is governed by common law in one of the Restatement areas, you can use the Restatement to find a statement of the common law rule, illustrations of the application of the rule, and cases in your jurisdiction that have cited the Restatement. The current Restatement areas are agency, conflict of laws, contracts, employment law, foreign relations, law governing lawyers, property, restitution, security, suretyship and guaranty, torts, trusts, unfair competition, and international commercial arbitration.

The Restatements are published by the American Law Institute after extensive study and revision and are edited by noted scholars, called *Reporters*. The original goal of the Restatements was to produce a coherent statement of the common law that would have the weight of primary authority. Later, this goal was changed to allow drafters to predict the law based on emerging trends, not just to summarize existing law. Therefore, you cannot rely on the Restatements to provide a statement of the law in your jurisdiction. Your jurisdiction may be more progressive than the Restatement; it may have adopted one Restatement rule but not another, closely related rule. Always do further research into the law of your jurisdiction.

B. Locating and Using Applicable Restatement Sections and Cases Citing Them

Sometimes another source or case will lead directly to a Restatement section on point. If you do not have a citation, you must first decide which subject governs your issue and then which series you should use.

To date, Restatements have been published in three series, which do not all cover the same areas. For example, one of the subjects in the Third series, the Restatement (Third) of the Law of Unfair Competition, was not treated as a separate topic in any of the earlier series.

In general, you will probably rely on the most recent series that addresses your topic. The original Restatements were published 50 or more years ago, and even in areas such as contracts and torts are less likely to help you understand the current state of the law than later series. However, you should not rule them out altogether.

If you are using Westlaw or Lexis Advance, look in the general content category *Secondary Sources* (Westlaw) or *Secondary Materials* (Lexis Advance). The Restatements are located in the specific category *Restatements*. Once in the specific category, you can keyword search all of the Restatements at once or select the specific Restatement covering the area of law you are researching.

Once in a specific Restatement, you can full-text keyword search, use the index, or use the table of contents.

Each print series includes topic volumes and index or appendix volumes. The volumes often have a similar appearance. Therefore, you need to pay close attention to which volume you are using, as well as which series you are using.[9]

Finding a specific Restatement section requires a different approach depending on the series you are using. A General Index covers the subjects in the First Restatement, but not subsequent series. The Second and Third Series have no comprehensive index. Instead, you must look in one of two places: the front of each topic volume generally has a table of contents, and the final topic volume in each subject generally has an index of that subject. Remember to check both places.

Once you have located a pertinent Restatement rule, you should read the comments and illustrations that follow each black letter rule. The comments may tell you, among other things, the intended scope of the rule; whether the rule reflects a consensus view or a modern trend; and whether there are other applicable Restatement sections. The illustrations, some of which are based on reported cases, will apply the rule to specific facts.

In addition to comments and illustrations, the Second and Third Series include Reporter's Notes for each section, which contain background information and citations to authority on which the drafters relied. Depending on the subject and series, these notes may appear in Appendix volumes instead of topic volumes.

C. The Role of Restatements in Your Research

You will probably use the Restatements for their black letter rules and as research tools for finding primary authority. Some situations allow you to use them as authority when writing to a court. As you research the application of your Restatement section, you may find that it has been adopted by your jurisdiction. In this instance only, you can cite the Restatement as authoritative.

---

9. Also shelved with the three Restatement series are Tentative Drafts. Prior to being approved by the American Law Institute, each Restatement goes through a series of drafts. The process can take years; some drafts are never approved or are approved only in part. The drafts are published with the notation T.D. and are occasionally cited by the courts. The second and third series include Conversion Tables that indicate where a section in a Tentative Draft appears in the final Restatement, assuming the draft is adopted.

You should cite the case that adopted the Restatement section, but you can use the Restatement as additional authority. You may also find that courts have cited a section approvingly without adopting it. In that case, you should continue to look for primary authority on point.

D. Updating Restatements

Restatements themselves are not updated. Although they are published in different series, a later series does not necessarily supersede a specific rule in an earlier series. If a court in your state has adopted a certain Restatement section as the law of that state, it will continue to be the law even if a subsequent version of the Restatement omits or alters its statement of the rule, unless the same court later explicitly adopts the newer version in place of the older one.

Print Restatements are supplemented by a sometimes confusing system of Appendix volumes along with bound and paper supplements. For this reason, you might prefer to go online for updating purposes, even if you read the black letter rules and comments in print. The following text describes the tools that are available for updating in print sources.

Originally, the Restatements were supplemented with a separate set of bound volumes entitled Restatements in the Courts, which was published in 1944 and supplemented annually through 1975 with bound volumes. The Second and Third Series, however, are supplemented with bound Appendix volumes for each subject. These volumes contain case digests giving a brief synopsis of each case that has cited a particular section so that you can determine not only how the section was treated, but also whether the case might be relevant to your research issue. To thoroughly research a particular section, therefore, you will need to gather several volumes: the Restatement topic volumes, any bound Appendix volumes, and any supplemental bound or paper volumes.

When using Appendix volumes, keep in mind that one volume generally contains references to more than one Restatement series. For example, the same Appendix volume may refer to both the Restatement of Torts and the Restatement (Second) of Torts. Pay close attention to the series and section number references on each page when using Appendix volumes to be sure you are retrieving cases that cite the correct section. The Appendix volumes are, in turn, supplemented with pocket parts and with a paper volume entitled Interim Case Citations, which contains citations but not case digests. You can find relatively recent cases this way, but you may need to check in several places.

Alternatively, KeyCite and Shepard's will allow you to determine whether any section of a Restatement has been cited by state or federal courts or by one of a small group of law reviews; however, they do not include treatment for Restatement sections. Courts can, among other things, adopt, reject, discuss, disapprove, or merely cite Restatement sections; you will have to check each case yourself to find the treatment.

Chapter 9

Practice Materials

Practice materials are specialized types of secondary sources. They are written for practicing attorneys, and they cover the substance and skills of the day-to-day practice of law. Examples of practice materials include sample forms, model clauses, looseleafs, checklists, bar journals, legal newspapers, and continuing legal education materials. As with any secondary source, practice materials discuss, describe or comment on the law, without having the force of law themselves. They also provide citations to relevant primary authority. The difference between practice materials and other legal secondary sources is the target audience. Because practice materials are written for (and often by) those involved in the practice of law, their focus is on what the law is and how to navigate it, rather than theoretical arguments about what the law should be.

After covering general principles on using practice materials, this chapter details several types of legal practice materials. These practical resources are a must for practicing attorneys, but they can also be of great value to self-represented/pro se litigants and others seeking to better understand a particular area of the law.

I. Using Practice Materials in General

Practice materials are the go-to secondary source for most practicing attorneys. They target narrow areas of the law, and they often do so in specific jurisdictions. For example, the best starting point for research on child custody in any state will almost always be a practice set written for that particular jurisdiction.

There are many types of practice materials. They range from short and simple overviews to very dense publications designed to cover every aspect of a subject. Practice materials exist for all areas of law, but they are especially concentrated in subject areas such as family law, real estate, criminal law, tort law, estate planning, and employee benefits. When you need examples of a document you are drafting for the first time, a checklist of what you need to allege to have a viable cause of action, or a quick summary of current developments in a particular area of the law, practice materials will often be your best resource.

A significant challenge in secondary source research is selecting the best source. Knowing you need to use practice materials is only the first step, as there are many different practice-oriented materials available to the legal researcher. With experience, you will learn which sources to select for particular types of issues. When you are new to legal research or a particular subject, however, it is best to ask for recommendations from a law librarian or a mentor you trust. You may also wish to review a web-based legal research guide for assistance in identifying relevant and trustworthy practice-oriented sources for a particular topic or jurisdiction.

Unlike primary legal materials, which are widely available through both high-cost electronic databases and the free web, the vast majority of practice materials are only available via a paid subscription. This is because their authors and publishers assert copyright in their works and only offer access to these specialized materials for a fee.

In addition, most practice-oriented titles are often available only through a single publisher or legal research platform (most often Westlaw, Lexis Advance, or Bloomberg Law), and the publisher charges a premium due to the exclusivity of the content. To try to keep costs down, some legal employers choose to purchase certain practice materials exclusively in print.

Finally, some legal researchers simply prefer to use practice materials in print. The printed page may simply feel more readable than a computer screen, with fewer visual distractions and a friendlier layout and font.

Whatever drives your use of practice materials in print, remember to pay especially close attention to how current a source is when using a print version of the source. Many print resources are not updated as quickly or as frequently as their electronic equivalents. Print sources will include their original publication date, but be sure to check for a more recent update either within the volume or in a separate supplement at the end of the set. When using an electronic source, this information is available in the scope note for the resource, which is typically accessible via a lower-case "i" with a circle around it. In either format, it is your responsibility to do an especially careful review of the time between the date of publication and the present.

Some practice materials can be updated using an online citator, like KeyCite on Westlaw or Shepard's on Lexis Advance. The resulting list of citing references will provide you with information about when the publication was cited to in other materials, such as a court opinion or another secondary source. If a source has been heavily cited to by other sources, especially primary legal authorities, this can be a clue that it is a well-respected publication. Note that not all practice materials can be checked using a citator, but it is an important avenue to consider, when possible, in determining whether the source you found reflects the current state of the law.

Most often, however, you will have to update the primary sources you find in practice materials using KeyCite or Shepard's.

II. Legal Looseleafs:
The Quintessential Practice Source

A. Overview

Legal looseleafs are the quintessential practice source for heavily regulated areas of the law, including tax, securities, labor, environmental, immigration, and the like. Looseleafs include both primary authority and secondary authority in a single resource. They combine extensive commentary with full reproductions of relevant statutes, regulations, and court opinions (both judicial opinions and agency decisions). As such, looseleafs are often seen as "one-stop shopping" in these practice areas, as they are the primary sets such practitioners turn to each day.

As one example, tax law research relies heavily on looseleaf services. To research a particular section of the Internal Revenue Code (IRC), most tax practitioners begin with a major tax looseleaf like *CCH's Standard Federal Tax Reporter*, rather than an annotated federal statute. This looseleaf is organized by IRC section and pulls together all relevant materials related to that section, including Treasury Department regulations, U.S. Tax Court decisions, I.R.S. guidance documents, legislative history materials, and expansive commentary.

The name "looseleaf" stems from the print publication scheme, although looseleafs are now widely available in electronic format. In the past, looseleafs were printed in three-ring "looseleaf binders." This format allowed for much faster updating, as libraries could simply crack open the binders and substitute pages as needed. Also, the publishers could send new, updated pages to add or revise information, rather than having to publish a whole new volume or set.

B. Finding Legal Looseleafs

A gateway issue in using legal looseleafs is identifying a relevant looseleaf in the first place. Especially in a world of online materials, where everything looks so similar, identifying the looseleafs available in a given subject area or for a particular jurisdiction can be challenging. Also, if a given looseleaf is only available on Westlaw, Lexis Advance or Bloomberg Law (or another legal platform), researchers need to be able to find it without browsing the secondary content on every potentially relevant platform.

Specific publications for identifying legal looseleafs address these challenges. The most prominent is *Legal Looseleafs: Electronic and Print*, which is published by Infosources Publishing. It is available in print as well as electronically through the LawTRIO database, and it includes over 2,600 looseleafs by over 100 publishers. *Legal Looseleafs: Electronic and Print* has multiple access points, including by subject, by publisher, and by electronic format type.

Online research guides are another resource source for identifying looseleafs. Prepared and posted to the web by academic law librarians, these guides focus on legal subjects, legal jurisdictions, and legal skill sets. In addition to listing available resources (including looseleafs), legal research guides often provide value judgments about various resources. You can rely on a law librarian's expertise to tell you which looseleafs are the strongest ones for a particular subject or jurisdiction.

To find a legal research guide, simply search the web for *legal research guide* along with the relevant subject area or jurisdiction. If several guides appear in the results list, choose to review one or more from the institutions you trust the most. If you are looking for a jurisdictional legal research guide, try to select one from an academic law library within that jurisdiction. For example, there are several strong legal research guides by law libraries in Pennsylvania, and they will point users to key Pennsylvania looseleafs, including a variety of titles by the local legal publisher George T. Bisel Company, Inc.

Whether using them electronically or in print, most researchers need practice to gain proficiency and comfort with legal looseleafs. Looseleafs can be challenging to learn to use because of their complexity and their sheer size. (As just one example, the *CCH's Standard Federal Tax Reporter*, referenced above, is 25 volumes in print.) While the organization of looseleafs varies by publication, most are organized by topic, by type of source, and/or by date. In addition, the vast majority of looseleafs, whether electronic or print, have a topical index to facilitate access to sections by subject as well as a "Help" or "How to Use" section to aid researchers. *Use these.* They can be a lifesaver.

One final organizational consideration to note is that most looseleafs rely on paragraph or section numbers, rather than page numbers. Any page numbers you see are there solely to guide print updates so newer material can replace older material without triggering the renumbering of the entire volume. As a researcher, the page numbers are meaningless. Ignore them and use paragraph numbers or section numbers instead. Even though the page numbers will change with future updates, the paragraph or section references will remain the same. Note, also, that looseleaf publishers use the term "paragraph" loosely. A paragraph may be just a few sentences, several actual paragraphs, or many pages in length.

III. Legal Forms

A. Overview

Legal forms are samples of specific types of legal documents. They are often published in "form books," but they can also appear in legal looseleafs, treatises, court rules, and continuing legal education materials. Depending on the source, there may also be checklists, case citations, and commentary on how such language has been interpreted in a particular jurisdiction. Note that sample language for specific clauses in a legal document is also available if you are looking for some guidance but do not need a full form.

Legal forms are a good tool to consult when you are drafting a document for the first time, whether it is a litigation document (e.g., a motion to dismiss or a motion to compel discovery) or a transactional document (e.g., a lease, a contract for the sale of property, or a will). Litigation forms are often referred to as "pleading and practice" forms in book titles and descriptions.

Legal forms can help a researcher by providing boilerplate language examples, setting forth options for non-boilerplate language, showing how something is formatted, and operating as a checklist of sorts to ensure nothing is omitted by mistake. In addition, commercial form sets with annotations often describe why certain clauses are necessary and let a researcher know which party a particular clause favors, such as whether it is pro-purchaser or pro-seller.

Be cautious when using forms, however. Legal forms are written for general audiences, and individual forms should only be used as a starting point. Many forms contain archaic language or unnecessary legalese. Unless you are using a form that is required by statute or approved by a court in your jurisdiction, try to eliminate any archaic or surplus language in favor of using plain English.

Also, be sure to carefully tailor sample legal forms to your client's needs, and consult more than one if you can to ensure you are not missing anything.

B. Finding Legal Forms

There are many ways to find legal forms, including online legal research guides for forms. Simply search for *legal research guide forms*, either alone or with the relevant legal document name, jurisdiction, and/or subject area. Online legal research guides for particular subject areas or jurisdictions may also have a section on forms, they may reference specific form books, or they may point to other access points to forms in the guide's secondary sources section.

Many form sets can also be found using a law library's online catalog. Simply look for a big search box or a hyperlink from the law library's website and run a basic search or a more targeted advanced search, depending on what you need.

Do not underestimate the value in consulting another person for assistance. A professional colleague, a law school professor, or a law librarian are all good examples of people to consult for advice on which legal forms are available and how to locate them. In addition, many law firms and other legal employers use internal document management systems to house their electronic work product, and these systems can be searched to find example legal documents drafted by colleagues at the same employer. Make sure you trust the sample document and its author before using it, though, and you should confirm with its author if any content was added and omitted based on the facts of the other matter.

Finally, major legal databases like Westlaw, Lexis Advance, Bloomberg Law, and others have entire sections on forms, which researchers can browse or search, and many of these forms can be filled out online and then downloaded or vice versa. Browsing for relevant legal forms can be more forgiving than searching, and it often provides the researcher with a more complete picture of what is available. When searching for legal forms in a new area, do not include too many search terms or otherwise be too narrow in your query, as it could exclude relevant materials. Instead, focus broadly and then narrow as you work your way through the results. If you are certain you know the correct terminology, then you can consider using advanced search techniques like terms and connectors (Boolean searching) to reduce the number of irrelevant results.

Note that many legal form sets are multi-jurisdictional or national in scope. Examples of form sets of this type focused on litigation forms include *American*

Jurisprudence Legal Forms 2d (Westlaw), *Nichols Cyclopedia of Legal Forms An-notated* (Westlaw), and *West's Legal Forms* (Westlaw). Examples of forms sets of this type focused on transactional forms include *Current Legal Forms with Tax Analysis (Rabkin & Johnson)* (Lexis Advance) and the drafting resources under the "Corporate Transactions" tab on Bloomberg Law, which include sample documents and clauses as well as a "draft analyzer" which compares a researcher's proposed language to the market.

Many legal form sets are specific to a particular jurisdiction. The primary form sets in Pennsylvania are *Dunlap-Hanna Pennsylvania Forms* (Lexis Advance), which includes both litigation and transactional forms; *Goodrich-Amram 2d* (Westlaw), which focuses on procedural rules with accompanying forms; *Pennsylvania Transaction Guide: Legal Forms* (Lexis Advance), which includes only transactional forms; and *West's Pennsylvania Forms* (Westlaw), which includes both litigation and transactional forms. In addition, *West's Pennsylvania Practice Series* (Westlaw), a practice-focused treatise set, has useful forms embedded within its treatise content.

Pennsylvania also has certain forms available on the free web via state government websites. For example, the website for Pennsylvania's Unified Judicial System[1] contains a variety of forms, including a series of complaints and other litigation forms as well as additional forms related to dependency, juvenile delinquency, court administration, and law enforcement. Forms are organized by category, which makes browsing very easy. The litigation forms are in the "for the public" category.

Lastly, numerous form sets are dedicated to Federal practice in the United States, including *American Jurisprudence Pleading and Practice Forms* (Westlaw), *Bender's Federal Practice Forms* (Lexis Advance), *Nichols Cyclopedia of Federal Procedure Forms* (Westlaw), and *West's Federal Forms* (Westlaw).

While model jury instructions, sample interrogatories, and other related practice tools are not technically legal forms in the same strict sense as the materials discussed above, they are worth mentioning because they can provide much of the same information as a legal form. Many of them can serve as a sample standing alone, and they can also serve as checklists for what must be proven to support a particular cause of action. In Pennsylvania, the Pennsylvania Bar Institute[2] publishes both *Pennsylvania Suggested Civil Jury Instructions* and *Pennsylvania Suggested Criminal Jury Instructions* as approved jury instructions for specific civil causes of action or criminal offenses. Both titles are avail-

---

1. (www.pacourts.us).
2. (www.pbi.org).

able on both Westlaw and Lexis Advance. Other key resources in this category include *American Jurisprudence Proof of Facts* (Westlaw), *Benders Forms of Discovery* (Lexis Advance), *Causes of Action* (Westlaw), and *Federal Jury Practice and Instructions* (Westlaw).

IV. CLE Materials

A. Overview

Continuing Legal Education (CLE) materials are another type of practice materials. CLE is professional education for attorneys who have already been admitted to the bar. A certain number of CLE credits are mandatory in most jurisdictions during each reporting period, including Pennsylvania, but there are no nationwide requirements. CLE instructors are typically experienced attorneys, judges, or law professors. National, state, and local bar associations all offer opportunities for CLE, as do a variety of other legal associations and groups.

CLE materials are prepared and distributed in conjunction with CLE courses, either electronically or in print. CLE materials are written by and for practitioners, so they have a very practical focus. These materials can be extensive, but that is not always the case, and they are prepared for readers with varying levels of experience and expertise. CLE materials are excellent resources for learning about a developing area of the law. Often a significant statute or case in a particular jurisdiction will be the subject of a CLE course within a few months of its enactment or decision.

B. Finding CLE Materials

Two of the largest CLE publishers nationwide are the Practising Law Institute (PLI) and the American Law Institute Continuing Legal Education Group (ALI CLE). The *PLI PLUS* database, available by subscription, includes PLI's treatises, course handbooks, answer books, legal forms, and program transcripts. These materials provide practical guidance for attorneys, and they are especially strong for transactional practice. In addition, Bloomberg Law contains limited PLI treatises. The ALI CLE courses and materials include online courses and live webcasts, as well as on-demand electronic publications, presented by prominent lawyers, judges and academics.[3]

---

3. The ALI CLE courses and materials are available for purchase at www.ali-cle.org.

Locally, the Pennsylvania Bar Institute (PBI) is the CLE arm of the Pennsylvania Bar Association, and PBI publishes Pennsylvania-specific CLE materials and practice guides on a wide variety of subjects. PBI includes a series of publications designed to complement its live CLE courses and on-demand offerings. These publications cover sixteen different major practice areas, are updated regularly, often include forms, and are available both in print and as e-books. In addition, the Philadelphia Bar Association is a statewide CLE provider in Pennsylvania, New Jersey, and Delaware.

A number of CLE publications and practice tools are available on Westlaw, Lexis Advance, and Bloomberg Law. The primary advantage of these versions is that they allow for full-text searching, but they are not as comprehensive as the other options discussed above and their coverage differs by platform.

When searching for and using CLE materials, there are a few important points to keep in mind. First, all of the major CLE providers allow users to search by subject or for a specific title, but you will not be able to access the full text without either a subscription to a commercial database or the purchase of a particular title in print or electronic form. Remember that local law libraries may be able to provide you with this access. Second, you must pay attention to how current the CLE materials are. Some CLE providers update their materials, but many do not change the materials until a new program on the same topic takes place. Third, some CLE materials provide only broad overviews while others include a very detailed examination of an area of the law. Expect a wide range of CLE materials, and do your best to select the one that works best for you in terms of depth of treatment. Finally, because CLE materials often highlight developing areas of the law, you should always check for relevant CLE materials on point if your research project involves interpreting a recent statute or case, examining an area that is subject to changing regulations, or analyzing a rapidly evolving area.

V. Practice-Focused Legal Periodicals

A. Overview

Legal periodicals publish articles on every aspect of the law, with their emphasis ranging from the extremely theoretical to the solidly practical. Practice-focused legal periodicals are the practical end of this spectrum, and they include bar journals, legal newspapers, and other current awareness publications. These practical publications typically have more frequent publication schedules than most scholarly works, and they are designed to provide clear overviews of the current state of the law for actively practicing attorneys. They also highlight new developments and identify evolving areas to make it easier to stay on top of these changes. Practice materials are almost always written by actively practicing attorneys who are experts in their area of specialization.

B. Finding Practice-Focused Legal Periodicals

Finding out which practice-focused legal periodicals exist in your jurisdiction and/or your practice area is step one to using these materials successfully. If you are already a member of a state bar association, some of these materials will come to you automatically. If you already have a legal job or are in law school, word of mouth is an excellent option. Ask a mentor, a work colleague, a professor, or a law librarian for recommendations. Jurisdiction-specific legal research guides are another excellent place to start. Simply search for *legal research guide* along with the relevant jurisdiction or subject area, and then find one that discusses the available practice-focused materials.

In Pennsylvania, the Pennsylvania Bar Association (PBA) publishes *The Pennsylvania Lawyer* magazine, the *Pennsylvania Bar News*, and the *Pennsylvania Bar Association Quarterly*. *The Pennsylvania Lawyer* magazine, published six times per year, includes practical "how-to" articles on practice-related trends and developments. The *Pennsylvania Bar News*, a newspaper published bi-weekly, includes brief summaries of new legal decisions and developments as well as other bar-related information. The *Pennsylvania Bar Association Quarterly*, the most scholarly of the PBA's publications, includes longer articles summarizing new legal developments in a scholarly style. Members can also sign up for PBA sections in particular practice areas, and most sections distribute subject-specific newsletters to their members. *The Pennsylvania Lawyer* magazine and the *Pennsylvania Bar Association Quarterly* are both available on Lexis Advance and Westlaw.

The Philadelphia Bar Association publishes the *Philadelphia Lawyer* and the *Philadelphia Bar Reporter*. The *Philadelphia Lawyer*, a quarterly magazine, covers legal practice areas, technology, fiction, lifestyles, and book reviews. The *Philadelphia Bar Reporter*, a newspaper printed monthly, includes bar association news and activities as well as staff coverage of events and contributions by sections and committees. Both publications are available in print and online by subscription through the Philadelphia Bar Association's website. The Philadelphia Bar Association also publishes the *Bar Reporter Online*, a weekly e-news brief emailed with new updates between regular issues of the *Philadelphia Bar Reporter*. It is distributed to members and subscribers at no extra cost.

The Legal Intelligencer, published by ALM, is the legal newspaper serving Philadelphia. It was founded in 1843 and is the oldest daily-published legal newspaper. The *Pennsylvania Law Weekly*, also published by ALM, is distributed weekly and includes, among other items, full-text trial court opinions and accompanying analysis. Both papers are available in print as well as online through a subscription to ALM's Law.com platform.

In addition to these local publications, there are many other national publications attorneys use to stay on top of new, practice-focused legal developments. The American Bar Association publishes its flagship monthly publication, the *ABA Journal*, along with over one hundred additional specialty periodicals distributed through its sections, divisions, and forums. New blogs by individuals, legal employers, and legal news providers with this same type of information seem to pop up every day. Plus, the vast majority of legal information vendors offer their own selection of current awareness publications on a variety of subjects. Bloomberg BNA publishes a particularly strong set of current awareness newsletters in several highly regulated practice areas. They are available online through either BNA Online or Bloomberg Law.

Whether you look locally or nationally, there are more potentially helpful practice-driven periodicals available than one can easily monitor. As such, in addition to soliciting feedback or otherwise doing a careful study before deciding where to focus one's attention, it is important to consider your own style and format preferences. If you know you will not read a dense print publication on a regular basis, opt instead for smaller updates sent by email. Or set up electronic alerts in preferred databases so you only see articles meeting a strict set of search parameters. Finally, revisit your subscriptions periodically and adjust them as necessary to ensure you are getting the best possible benefit from practice-focused legal periodicals and current awareness tools.

Appendix

Legal Citation

I. Overview[1]

In a legal document, every legal rule and every explanation of the law must be cited. Legal citations are included in the text of legal documents rather than being saved for a bibliography. While you may initially feel that these citations clutter your document, you will soon learn to appreciate the valuable information that they provide. The format used to convey that information, however, requires attention to details regarding abbreviations, spacing, and font, among others. Rather than trying to understand why citations are formatted the way they are, the most practical approach is simply to learn citation rules and apply them. Frequent repetition will make them second nature.

The main sources of information on formatting legal citations are the two national citation manuals, the *ALWD Guide to Legal Citation*[2] and *The Bluebook: A Uniform System of Citation.*[3] In addition to these manuals, state statutes, court rules, and style manuals may dictate the form of citation used before the courts of different states. For Pennsylvania-specific citation conventions, students and practitioners should also refer to *PAstyle: A Pennsylvania Stylebook and Citation Guide for Legal Writing.*[4] Once you are aware of the basic function and format of citation, adapting to a slightly different set of rules is not difficult.

---

1. Portions of this chapter are drawn from *Oregon Legal Research*, by Suzanne E. Rowe, and are used with permission.

2. ALWD & Coleen M. Barger, *ALWD Guide to Legal Citation* (5th ed. 2014) ("*ALWD Guide*"). The sixth edition is expected soon after the release of this book, though no major changes are predicted.

3. *The Bluebook: A Uniform System of Citation* (20th ed. 2015) ("the *Bluebook*").

4. *PAstyle: A Pennsylvania Stylebook and Citation Guide for Legal Writing* (6th ed. 2016) ("*PAstyle*").

Table A-1. Purposes of Legal Citations

- Show the reader where to find the cited material in the original case, statute, rule, article, or other authority.
- Indicate the weight and persuasiveness of each authority, for example, by specifying the court that decided the case, the author of a document, and the publication date of the authority.
- Convey the type and degree of support the authority offers, for example, by indicating whether the authority supports your point directly or only implicitly.
- Demonstrate that the analysis in your document is the result of careful research.

Source: ALWD & Coleen M. Barger, *ALWD Guide to Legal Citation* 2 (5th ed. 2014) (*"ALWD Guide"*).

Citations not only tell readers where to find the authorities relied on in a legal document, but also convey information about how the authorities support the writer's analysis. This Appendix provides general guidance on how to use legal citations to support your analysis and identifies some special considerations to keep in mind when citing specific types of legal authority. Finally, the Appendix provides advice on editing citations.

Table A-1 lists the purposes of legal citation in documents.

A. The *ALWD Guide*

Of the two national citation manuals, the *ALWD Guide* is the best manual for novices. Citation formats in the *ALWD Guide* are organized by legal source, the explanations are clear, and the abundant examples are useful to both law students and practicing attorneys. Beginning with the fifth edition, the *ALWD Guide* also includes citation formats for academic footnotes, which are traditionally formatted differently from citations in briefs and memoranda. The differences between the *ALWD Guide* and the *Bluebook*, the other national citation manual, are differences in the presentation and explanation the manuals provide rather than differences in the technical format of the citations for specific sources.

B. The *Bluebook*

The other national citation manual is *The Bluebook: A Uniform System of Citation*, which is written by student editors of four Ivy League law reviews.

Until the *ALWD Guide* was first published in 2000, the *Bluebook* was the only national citation system that was widely recognized. Many law firms, agencies, and organizations still consider *Bluebook* citations the norm, although few practicing lawyers know its current rules; most assume that the *Bluebook* rules have not changed since they were in law school. Like the *ALWD Guide*, the *Bluebook* has two citation formats: a citation format for practice-based documents, such as legal memoranda and briefs, and a citation format for footnotes in academic publications. The *Bluebook*, however, emphasizes the style for academic publications. The rules most important to attorneys, those concerning practice-based documents, are covered in the Bluepages. The Bluepages is a section of the *Bluebook*, situated near the beginning of the book, which is easily identified by its literal blue pages.

Perhaps the most helpful information in the *Bluebook* are the reference guides on the inside covers of the book. The inside front cover provides examples of citations used in academic footnotes, and the inside back cover gives examples of citations in court documents and legal memoranda. Note that the examples in the remainder of the *Bluebook* are in the style used for academic footnotes. If you are writing a document other than a law review article, you will need to refer also to the Bluepages and the examples inside the back cover to see how you must modify the examples in the remainder of the *Bluebook*.

C. *PAstyle*

PAstyle: A Pennsylvania Stylebook and Citation Guide for Legal Writing provides comprehensive guidelines for citing Pennsylvania-specific legal sources. The purpose of *PAstyle* is to provide the Pennsylvania legal community with an easy-to-use style manual. However, *PAstyle* is not a replacement for the national citation manuals; it is not an exhaustive catalog of citation forms for different types of sources.[5] Instead, it supplements other manuals with the citation forms preferred by Pennsylvania courts and legal publications.

PAstyle discusses local procedural rules and provides specific examples of citations for Pennsylvania cases, statutes, rules of court, and local county rules.[6] In addition, federal authorities are covered, including case law, statutes and rules of court.[7] Finally, examples of federal and state constitutions, legislative materials, slip laws, and a selection of secondary sources are included.[8] Citation

---

5. *Id.* at xi.
6. *Id.* at 8–27.
7. *Id.* at 28–33.
8. *Id.* at 34–37.

Table A-2. Examples of Citation Sentences and Citation Clauses

Citation Sentence: Under Pennsylvania law, loss of consortium means loss by one spouse of whatever aid, assistance, comfort, and society one spouse would be expected to bestow upon the other. *Tucker v. Fischbein*, 237 F.3d 275, 290 (3d Cir. 2001).

Citation Clauses: The determination of marital property rights through a settlement agreement has long been permitted, and even encouraged, *Holz v. Holz*, 850 A.2d 751, 757 (Pa. Super. 2004), but terms of marital settlement agreements cannot be modified by a court in absence of a specific judicial modification provision within the agreement, *Stamerro v. Stamerro*, 889 A.2d 1251, 1258 (Pa. Super. 2005).

Academic Footnote: Under Pennsylvania law, loss of consortium means loss by one spouse of whatever aid, assistance, comfort, and society one spouse would be expected to bestow upon the other.[1]

1. Tucker v. Fischbein, 237 F.3d 275, 290 (3d Cir. 2001).

conventions are covered in a separate chapter of *PAstyle* and include rules governing topics such as abbreviations in citations, the use of short citations, commercial database cites, and parentheticals.[9]

II. Citation Basics

A. Incorporating Citations into a Document

You must provide a citation for each idea, legal principle, or quotation that comes from a case, statute, article, or other source. References to or descriptions of legal authority must also be cited. Thus, paragraphs that state legal rules and explain the law should contain many citations.

A citation may offer support for an entire sentence or for an idea expressed in part of a sentence. In practice-based documents, when a citation supports an entire sentence, it is placed in a separate *citation sentence* that begins with a capital letter and ends with a period. If a citation supports only a portion of the sentence, it is included immediately after the relevant part of that sentence and set off from the sentence by commas in what is called a *citation clause*. In a scholarly publication, such as a law review article, citations are placed in footnotes, instead of in the main text of the document. Table A-2 provides examples of each.

---

9. *Id.* at 39–55.

Table A-3. Common Signals

Signal	Explanation
No signal	The source cited provides direct support for the idea in the sentence, such as when you are paraphrasing a rule of law. Or, the citation identifies the source of a quotation.
E.g.,	Many authorities directly state the idea in the sentence, and you are citing only one or two as examples. Note: do not italicize the comma that follows the signal.
See	The source cited offers implicit support for the idea in the sentence.
See also	The source cited provides additional support for an idea that has already been discussed and cited to another source. This signal can be helpful, for example, when a case provides a slightly different illustration of a rule you have already discussed.

Source: *ALWD Guide* Rule 35.1.

In a memorandum, do not cite your client's facts or your conclusions about a case, statute, or other authority. For example, the following sentence should not be cited: "Under the facts presented, our client has a strong claim for loss of consortium." These facts and conclusions are unique to your situation and would not be found anywhere in the reference source. In a brief to a court, you will provide record cites for your client's facts.

B. Signals

A citation must show the reader the level of support each authority provides. You do this by deciding whether to use an introductory signal and, if so, which one. The more common signals are explained in Table A-3.

C. Explanatory Parentheticals

Additional information about an authority can be appended to its citation in parentheses. Sometimes this parenthetical information conveys to the reader the weight of the authority. For example, a case may have been decided *en banc* or *per curiam* ("by the court"). Or the case may have been decided by a narrow margin. Parenthetical information allows you to name the judges who joined in a dissenting, concurring, or plurality opinion.

An explanatory parenthetical can convey helpful, additional information about the authority in a compressed space. It can, for instance, summarize the crucial facts or reasoning of a case or explain the relationship between two authorities. Explanatory parentheticals are generally not necessary when a source is cited with no signal or with *e.g.*, because in those cases the source should provide direct support for the proposition cited. When other signals are used, indicating more indirect support, an explanatory parenthetical can make clear how the source supports your analysis.

Parenthetical information generally should not be given in a complete sentence, but should begin with a present participle (i.e., a verb ending in "-ing") that is not capitalized. The exception is when a full sentence from an authority is quoted within an explanatory parenthetical.

> EXAMPLE: As a general rule, a plaintiff in a medical malpractice action in Pennsylvania is required to present testimony from a medical expert regarding the elements of duty, breach, and causation. *E.g.*, *Quinby v. Plumsteadville Family Practice*, 589 Pa. 183, 199, 907 A.2d 1061, 1070–71 (2006). When the plaintiff proves her injury is one that normally would not happen in the absence of negligence, however, the plaintiff can rely on the doctrine of res ipsa loquitur, which allows the jury to infer the defendant's negligence from the surrounding circumstances. *Id.* at 199–200, 907 A.2d at 1071. For example, in *Quinby*, the court held a res ipsa loquitur jury instruction was warranted when a quadriplegic patient was left unattended on an examination table and fell. *Id.* at 202, 907 A.2d at 1072–73; *see also Fessenden v. Robert Packer Hosp.*, 97 A.3d 1225, 1233 (Pa. Super. 2014) (allowing plaintiff to rely on res ipsa loquitur to establish elements of a malpractice claim when a surgical sponge was left in plaintiff's abdomen after an operation).

D. Quotations

In legal documents, quotations should be used only when the reader needs to see the text exactly as it appears in the original authority. For example, quoting controlling statutory language is often necessary. If a judicial opinion summarizes or explains an analytical point in a particularly insightful way, a quotation may be warranted.

Excessive quotation has two drawbacks. First, excessive use of quotations may suggest to the reader that you do not fully comprehend the material; it is much easier to cut and paste together a document from pieces of various cases than to synthesize and explain a rule of law. Second, quotations interrupt the flow of your writing when the style of the quoted language differs from your own.

When you decide a quotation is needed, the words, punctuation, and capitalization within the quotation marks must appear *exactly* as they are in the original. Any alterations or omissions must be indicated. Include commas and periods inside quotation marks; place other punctuation outside the quotation marks unless it is included in the original text. A citation to the source must immediately follow the quotation.

When a quotation is fifty or more words, single-space the quotation, and indent it by one tab from both the right and left margins. Do not place quotation marks around a block quotation. Instead, to separate the block quotation from the surrounding text, insert a blank line before and after the block quote. The citation for the quoted material should not be placed within the block of text; place it on the next line following the block quotation, beginning at the left margin.

E. Short Forms

Once you have cited an authority in full, you do not need to repeat the full citation within the same general discussion. Different authorities have different "short forms," which are described in detail in the national citation manuals.

The short form for a case is typically the first party's name (unless the first party is "Commonwealth" or "State," in which case the second party's name is used), followed by the reporter volume, the word "at," and the appropriate page number. Do not omit the volume number; this is one of the most common errors in short citations.

Id. is an acceptable short form for almost any type of primary or secondary authority, as long as it is used to refer back to the immediately preceding citation. If the authority is cited using specific page numbers, then the short form will include the word "at" before the page number, followed by a page number, unless you are citing exactly the same page number cited in the preceding citation.

EXAMPLES:

Fessenden v. Robert Packer Hosp., 97 A.3d 1225 (Pa. Super. 2014).

Fessenden, 97 A.3d at 1233.

Id. at 1234.

23 Pa. Cons. Stat. Ann. § 3323 (West 2016).

Id. § 3324.

The word "*supra*" can also be used to refer back to most secondary authorities. *Supra* is not used to refer to cases, statutes, or regulations. As with "*id.*," if the source you are citing is cited by specific page number, the short form will include the word "at" followed by a page number.

EXAMPLES:

Amy E. Sloan, *Researching the Law: Finding What You Need When You Need It* 7 (2014).

Sloan, *supra* at 58.

21 Charles Alan Wright & Arthur R. Miller, *Federal Practice and Procedure* § 1006 (2d ed. 1987).

Wright & Miller, *supra* § 1005.

III. Special Considerations for Specific Legal Authorities and Sources

A. Case Citations

Pinpoint references. When citing a judicial opinion, you should provide a specific page reference to the point within the opinion that supports your analysis. This is called a "pinpoint" reference or "pincite." The first full citation to a case will normally include both the first page of the case and the pinpoint page reference, separated by a comma and a space. If the pinpoint page you are citing is also the first page of the case, then the same page number will appear twice. When using an online version of a case, remember that a reference to a specific reporter page may change in the middle of a computer screen or a printed page. This means that the page number indicated at the top of the screen or printed page may not be the page where the relevant information is located. For example, if the notation *275 appeared in the text before the relevant information, the pinpoint cite would be to page 275, not page 274.

Parallel citations. In jurisdictions where cases are published in more than one reporter, such as Pennsylvania Supreme Court cases, you will often need to provide a parallel citation for each reporter. To determine whether parallel citations are required in a particular jurisdiction, check the local rules, which are referenced in the *ALWD Guide* Appendices and *Bluebook* Tables.

The official reporter should be placed first in a parallel cite. Provide a pinpoint reference to pages in the official reporter; additional pinpoint references are optional, but usually appreciated.

In the date parenthetical, you may omit any part of the court abbreviation, if the name of the court can be clearly determined from the reporter abbreviation or the name of the database. Thus, because the reporter abbreviation

"Pa." indicates the decision was from the Pennsylvania Supreme Court, no court designation is needed in the date parenthetical.

Do not use *id.* alone as a short citation for a parallel cite. *Id.* only refers to a single source. However, if local court rules allow, you may use *id.* to refer to the first source in a parallel citation. For the second source, or any other subsequent sources, provide the volume number, reporter abbreviation, and pinpoint page reference. Place a comma and one space at the end of the short citation to the first source, followed by the volume number, reporter abbreviation, the word "at," and the pinpoint reference for the second source.

EXAMPLES:

Hiller v. Fausey, 588 Pa. 342, 348, 904 A.2d 875, 879 (2006).

Id. at 353, 904 A.2d at 882.

Prior and subsequent history. Sometimes a citation needs to show what happened to a judicial opinion at an earlier or later stage of litigation. The case you are citing may have affirmed an earlier decision, as in the example below. Or, you may decide to include a discussion of a case that was later overruled; in that instance, your reader needs to know the subsequent history as soon as you introduce the case.[10]

EXAMPLE: Juries in medical malpractice cases should not be instructed that physicians cannot be held liable for "errors in judgment" because that type of instruction has such a high risk of creating confusion about the standard of care. *Passarello v. Grumbine*, 87 A.3d 285, 304 (Pa. 2014), *aff'g* 29 A.3d 1158 (Pa. Super. 2011).

B. Statutes and Constitutions

The general rule that official codes should be cited whenever possible is not always possible to follow. In federal research, the *United States Code* is published so slowly that the current language of a statutory provision will most likely be found online or in one of the annotated codes in print. The authenticated online version of the code is the Government Publishing Office's Federal Digital System ("FDsys") version. An authenticated federal statute on FDsys should be cited to the *United States Code*. In some situations, current statutory language

---

10. A situation where you might cite a case that was later overruled is the situation where you are citing a case for a court's analysis of one issue and a later court reversed only on the second issue. Sometimes a lower court opinion will refer to specific facts that are not repeated in a later opinion, but which are helpful to include in your discussion, even if the lower court's holding is reversed.

may have to be cited to *United States Code Annotated* (U.S.C.A., published by West) or *United States Code Service* (U.S.C.S., published by LexisNexis).

EXAMPLES:

(statutory language appears in both the bound volume and the supplement) 29 U.S.C.A. § 1132 (West 2009 & Supp. 2016).

(statutory language appears in just the supplement) 18 U.S.C.A. § 2X7.1 (West Supp. 2016).

(statutory language appears in a commercial database) 29 U.S.C.A. § 1132 (Thomson Reuters Westlaw through Pub. L. No. 114-254).

Similar citing issues arise when citing Pennsylvania statutes because of the unique combination of official and unofficial statutes.

EXAMPLES:

(statutory language in a print volume) 23 Pa. Cons. Stat. Ann. § 3323 (West 2016).

(statutory language in a commercial database) 23 Pa. Cons. Stat. § 3323 (Lexis Advance through Act 174 of 2016 Reg. Sess.).

A constitutional provision that is currently in force should typically be cited to a print source. Use roman numerals when citing articles and amendments in the United States Constitution. However, Arabic numbers should be used for subsections and clauses. To cite a state constitution, follow the numbering system set forth within the cited source.

When citing a constitutional provision that has been published in a commercial database, add a parenthetical identifying the database. Within the parenthetical, include the "currency" of the constitutional provision, as indicated by the commercial database. No parenthetical is needed when citing a constitutional provision that has been published, edited or compiled online under the supervision of government officials. Instead, cite the online provision as you would cite the print version.

EXAMPLES:

U.S. Const, amend I.

Pa. Const. art. III, § 1.

U.S. Const, amend I (Lexis Advance through PL 114-248, approved 11/28/16).

Pa. Const. art. III, § 1 (Bloomberg Law through 2014).

C. Secondary Sources

Your first choice of authority should always be a primary source, if you can find one on point. Secondary sources can be cited for background material, for concise summaries of an area of the law, or as persuasive support—for example, when arguing that a rule of law has become outdated. In these situations, the secondary source will often be introduced with the signal "*see generally*" and the citation will include an explanatory parenthetical telling the reader why the source is helpful. Books, treatises, and periodicals can be cited in legal memos and briefs; Restatements of the Law, which can have high persuasive value in certain circumstances, might also be cited. Other secondary sources and practice materials are normally not cited, but are simply used as springboards for your research.

Each type of secondary source has its own very detailed citation conventions, which are described in the national citation manuals. When researching in secondary sources, take careful notes about the volume number, if any; title of the volume; author's name; title of the article or section you are using; whether the source is arranged by page number, paragraph number, or some other designation; the specific location of the information you may cite; the publisher; and the year of the volume. This information will help you draft accurate citations when you begin to draft your memo or brief, even if you are doing all of your research online.

The preferred citation form for a book, treatise, or other nonperiodic material is to the print version. However, if the work is solely available electronically or is difficult to obtain in print, you may place a comma after the full citation and add a commercial database's unique identifier or the Uniform Resource Locator (URL) for a reliable online location.

IV. Editing Citations

Ensuring that the citations in your document correctly reflect your research and support your analysis will require time, just like editing your writing. Be sure to leave enough time for both.

As you are researching, take careful notes about your sources. It is usually easier to gather all the information you need for a complete citation when you have recently read the source than to go back and find a specific point in one of your sources later. Then, as you are writing a legal document, refer frequently to the citation guide required by your supervisor or office.

Be extremely careful when cutting and pasting text from any source. If you do so, immediately put the text in quotation marks so that you will recognize it as a quote when you go back to edit your document. A judge or clerk who checks one of your citations and realizes that two lines of text in a brief were not just a paraphrase of another court's holding, but a direct quote, will be unimpressed at the very best, even if you have provided a citation to the case in question.

Check your citations a final time after you are finished editing the text of your document. Often a change in the text will affect the accuracy of a citation. For example, moving a sentence might require you to change an *id.* to another short citation form, or vice versa. In fact, some writers do not insert *id.* citations until they are completely finished writing and revising the text of a memo or brief. Also, sometimes a revision to the text will require a change to the signals introducing your citations. You might have no signal for a citation following a quotation in your draft, but then paraphrase the quotation during the editing process in a way that requires a signal. In this final editing stage, it can be helpful to highlight the citations in your document and then review them in order.

Using correct, complete citations will convey a level of attention to detail and professionalism which, in turn, will give your readers a sense that they can rely on your analysis. It is worth the time it takes to get your citations right.

About the Authors

Barbara J. Busharis is an assistant public defender, specializing in appeals, in Tallahassee, Florida. After graduating from NYU School of Law in 1991, she spent three years in the Philadelphia office of Duane, Morris & Heckscher (now Duane Morris). From 1994 through 2004 she taught legal writing and research at the Florida State University College of Law, and continues to be active with the moot court team there. In addition, she edits the *Trial Advocate Quarterly*, the journal of the Florida Defense Lawyers Association.

Catherine M. Dunn is the Director of the Law Library and Professor at the University of Denver Sturm College of Law. From 2015 through 2017 she was the Director of the Law Library and Associate Professor at Temple University's Beasley School of Law. Professor Dunn graduated from the University of Michigan Law School and the School of Information Sciences (the iSchool) at the University of Illinois, and she worked in the law library and taught legal research courses at Georgetown Law and the UConn School of Law before joining Temple. She also worked for six years as an associate for two law firms in Chicago and served as a judicial clerk for a justice on the Wisconsin Supreme Court.

Bonny L. Tavares is on the faculty of Temple University's Beasley School of Law, where she teaches appellate advocacy and legal research and writing, and also chairs the Moot Court Committee. A 1993 graduate of Howard University School of Law, she served as an Attorney Advisor for the United States Department of Housing and Urban Development from 1994 to 2000, where she specialized in labor and employment litigation. From 2000 to 2003, Professor Tavares taught legal research and writing at Howard University School of Law.

Carla P. Wale is the Head of Public Services at Temple University's Beasley School of Law Library. Prior to joining Temple, she held the positions of Reference Librarian at Georgetown University Law Center and Research and Electronic Technologies Librarian at Northern Illinois University College of Law.

She currently teaches advanced legal research courses at Temple and also taught at Georgetown Law and Northern Illinois University Law. She holds a J.D. from Loyola University College of Law and an M.L.I.S. with a certificate in Law Librarianship from the University of Washington.

Index